THE
CHUMASH

Robert O. Gibson

Frank W. Porter III
General Editor

CHELSEA HOUSE PUBLISHERS
New York   Philadelphia

On the cover A pair of pelican effigy stones made of steatite. The stones were probably used by the Chumash as fishing talismans.

Chelsea House Publishers
Editor-in-Chief Remmel Nunn
Managing Editor Karyn Gullen Browne
Copy Chief Juliann Barbato
Picture Editor Adrian G. Allen
Art Director Maria Epes
Deputy Copy Chief Mark Rifkin
Assistant Art Director Loraine Machlin
Manufacturing Manager Gerald Levine
Systems Manager Lindsey Ottman
Production Manager Joseph Romano
Production Coordinator Marie Claire Cebrián

Indians of North America
Senior Editor Liz Sonneborn

Staff for **THE CHUMASH**
Assistant Editor Claire Wilson
Copy Editor Joseph Roman
Editorial Assistant Michele Haddad
Designer Debora Smith
Picture Researcher Joan Beard

3 5 7 9 8 6 4

Library of Congress Cataloging-in-Publication Data

Gibson, Robert O.
The Chumash/by Robert O. Gibson
p. cm.—(Indians of North America)
Includes bibliographical references.
Summary: Examines the history, changing fortunes, and current situation of the Chumash Indians. Includes a photo essay on their crafts.
ISBN 1-55546-700-8
     0-7910-0376-0 (pbk.)
1. Chumashan Indians. [1. Chumashan Indians. 2. Indians of North America.] I. Title II. Series: Indians of North America (Chelsea House Publishers)   90-34776
E99.C815G53   1990   CIP
973'.04975—dc20   AC

CONTENTS

INDIANS OF NORTH AMERICA

CHELSEA HOUSE PUBLISHERS

INDIANS OF NORTH AMERICA: CONFLICT AND SURVIVAL

Frank W. Porter III

The Indians survived our open intention of wiping them out, and since the tide turned they have even weathered our good intentions toward them, which can be much more deadly.

John Steinbeck
America and Americans

When Europeans first reached the North American continent, they found hundreds of tribes occupying a vast and rich country. The newcomers quickly recognized the wealth of natural resources. They were not, however, so quick or willing to recognize the spiritual, cultural, and intellectual riches of the people they called Indians.

The Indians of North America examines the problems that develop when people with different cultures come together. For American Indians, the consequences of their interaction with non-Indian people have been both productive and tragic. The Europeans believed they had "discovered" a "New World," but their religious bigotry, cultural bias, and materialistic world view kept them from appreciating and understanding the people who lived in it. All too often they attempted to change the way of life of the indigenous people. The Spanish conquistadores wanted the Indians as a source of labor. The Christian missionaries, many of whom were English, viewed them as potential converts. French traders and trappers used the Indians as a means to obtain pelts. As Francis Parkman, the 19th-century historian, stated, "Spanish civilization crushed the Indian; English civilization scorned and neglected him; French civilization embraced and cherished him."

Nearly 500 years later, many people think of American Indians as curious vestiges of a distant past, waging a futile war to survive in a Space Age society. Even today, our understanding of the history and culture of American Indians is too often derived from unsympathetic, culturally biased, and inaccurate reports. The American Indian, described and portrayed in thousands of movies, television programs, books, articles, and government studies, has either been raised to the status of the "noble savage" or disparaged as the "wild Indian" who resisted the westward expansion of the American frontier.

Where in this popular view are the real Indians, the human beings and communities whose ancestors can be traced back to ice-age hunters? Where are the creative and indomitable people whose sophisticated technologies used the natural resources to ensure their survival, whose military skill might even have prevented European settlement of North America if not for devastating epidemics and disruption of the ecology? Where are the men and women who are today diligently struggling to assert their legal rights and express once again the value of their heritage?

The various Indian tribes of North America, like people everywhere, have a history that includes population expansion, adaptation to a range of regional environments, trade across wide networks, internal strife, and warfare. This was the reality. Europeans justified their conquests, however, by creating a mythical image of the New World and its native people. In this myth, the New World was a virgin land, waiting for the Europeans. The arrival of Christopher Columbus ended a timeless primitiveness for the original inhabitants.

Also part of this myth was the debate over the origins of the American Indians. Fantastic and diverse answers were proposed by the early explorers, missionairies, and settlers. Some thought that the Indians were descended from the Ten Lost Tribes of Israel, others that they were descended from inhabitants of the lost continent of Atlantis. One writer suggested that the Indians had reached North America in another Noah's ark.

A later myth, perpetrated by many historians, focused on the relentless persecution during the past five centuries until only a scattering of these "primitive" people remained to be herded onto reservations. This view fails to chronicle the overt and covert ways in which the Indians successfully coped with the intruders.

All of these myths presented one-sided interpretations that ignored the complexity of European and American events and policies. All left serious questions unanswered. What were the origins of the American Indians? Where did they come from? How and when did they get to the New World? What was their life—their culture—really like?

In the late 1800s, anthropologists and archaeologists in the Smithsonian Institution's newly created Bureau of American Ethnology in Washington,

D.C., began to study scientifically the history and culture of the Indians of North America. They were motivated by an honest belief that the Indians were on the verge of extinction and that along with them would vanish their languages, religious beliefs, technology, myths, and legends. These men and women went out to visit, study, and record data from as many Indian communities as possible before this information was forever lost.

By this time there was a new myth in the national consciousness. American Indians existed as figures in the American past. They had performed a historical mission. They had challenged white settlers who trekked across the continent. Once conquered, however, they were supposed to accept graciously the way of life of their conquerors.

The reality again was different. American Indians resisted both actively and passively. They refused to lose their unique identity, to be assimilated into white society. Many whites viewed the Indians not only as members of a conquered nation but also as "inferior" and "unequal." The rights of the Indians could be expanded, contracted, or modified as the conquerors saw fit. In every generation, white society asked itself what to do with the American Indians. Their answers have resulted in the twists and turns of federal Indian policy.

There were two general approaches. One way was to raise the Indians to a "higher level" by "civilizing" them. Zealous missionaries considered it their Christian duty to elevate the Indian through conversion and scanty education. The other approach was to ignore the Indians until they disappeared under pressure from the ever-expanding white society. The myth of the "vanishing Indian" gave stronger support to the latter option, helping to justify the taking of the Indians' land.

Prior to the end of the 18th century, there was no national policy on Indians simply because the American nation has not yet come into existence. American Indians similarly did not possess a political or social unity with which to confront the various Europeans. They were not homogeneous. Rather, they were loosely formed bands and tribes, speaking nearly 300 languages and thousands of dialects. The collective identity felt by Indians today is a result of their common experiences of defeat and/or mistreatment at the hands of whites.

During the colonial period, the British crown did not have a coordinated policy toward the Indians of North America. Specific tribes (most notably the Iroquois and the Cherokee) became military and political pawns used by both the crown and the individual colonies. The success of the American Revolution brought no immediate change. When the United States acquired new territory from France and Mexico in the early 19th century, the federal government wanted to open this land to settlement by homesteaders. But the Indian tribes that lived on this land had signed treaties with European governments assuring their title to the land. Now the United States assumed legal responsibility for honoring these treaties.

At first, President Thomas Jefferson believed that the Louisiana Purchase contained sufficient land for both the Indians and the white population. Within a generation, though, it became clear that the Indians would not be allowed to remain. In the 1830s the federal government began to coerce the eastern tribes to sign treaties agreeing to relinquish their ancestral land and move west of the Mississippi River. Whenever these negotiations failed, President Andrew Jackson used the military to remove the Indians. The southeastern tribes, promised food and transportation during their removal to the West, were instead forced to walk the "Trail of Tears." More than 4,000 men, woman, and children died during this forced march. The "removal policy" was successful in opening the land to homesteaders, but it created enormous hardships for the Indians.

By 1871 most of the tribes in the United States had signed treaties ceding most or all of their ancestral land in exchange for reservations and welfare. The treaty terms were intended to bind both parties for all time. But in the General Allotment Act of 1887, the federal government changed its policy again. Now the goal was to make tribal members into individual landowners and farmers, encouraging their absorption into white society. This policy was advantageous to whites who were eager to acquire Indian land, but it proved disastrous for the Indians. One hundred thirty-eight million acres of reservation land were subdivided into tracts of 160, 80, or as little as 40 acres, and allotted tribe members on an individual basis. Land owned in this way was said to have "trust status" and could not be sold. But the surplus land—all Indian land not allotted to individuals—was opened (for sale) to white settlers. Ultimately, more than 90 million acres of land were taken from the Indians by legal and illegal means.

The resulting loss of land was a catastrophe for the Indians. It was necessary to make it illegal for Indians to sell their land to non-Indians. The Indian Reorganization Act of 1934 officially ended the allotment period. Tribes that voted to accept the provisions of this act were reorganized, and an effort was made to purchase land within preexisting reservations to restore an adequate land base.

Ten years later, in 1944, federal Indian policy again shifted. Now the federal government wanted to get out of the "Indian business." In 1953 an act of Congress named specific tribes whose trust status was to be ended "at the earliest possible time." This new law enabled the United States to end unilaterally, whether the Indians wished it or not, the special status that protected the land in Indian tribal reservations. In the 1950s federal Indian policy was to transfer federal responsibility and jurisdiction to state governments,

10

encourage the physical relocation of Indian peoples from reservations to urban areas, and hasten the termination, or extinction, of tribes.

Between 1954 and 1962 Congress passed specific laws authorizing the termination of more than 100 tribal groups. The stated purpose of the termination policy was to ensure the full and complete integration of Indians into American society. However, there is a less benign way to interpret this legislation. Even as termination was being discussed in Congress, 133 separate bills were introduced to permit the transfer of trust land ownership from Indians to non-Indians.

With the Johnson administration in the 1960s the federal government began to reject termination. In the 1970s yet another Indian policy emerged. Known as "self-determination," it favored keeping the protective role of the federal government while increasing tribal participation in, and control of, important areas of local government. In 1983 President Reagan, in a policy statement on Indian affairs, restated the unique "government is government" relationship of the United States with the Indians. However, federal programs since then have moved toward transferring Indian affairs to individual states, which have long desired to gain control of Indian land and resources.

As long as American Indians retain power, land, and resources that are coveted by the states and the federal government, there will continue to be a "clash of cultures," and the issues will be contested in the courts, Congress, the White House, and even in the international human rights community. To give all Americans a greater comprehension of the issues and conflicts involving American Indians today is a major goal of this series. These issues are not easily understood, nor can these conflicts be readily resolved. The study of North American Indian history and culture is a necessary and important step toward that comprehension. All Americans must learn the history of the relations between the Indians and the federal government, recognize the unique legal status of the Indians, and understand the heritage and cultures of the Indians of North America.

Chumash elder Rafael Solares, photographed in 1877 by the French scientist Leon de Cessac, who excavated many Chumash sites during the late 1870s. Cessac posed Solares in the traditional clothing and body decoration—a feathered headdress, a cord skirt, and painted-on rings—of a member of the Chumash antap *cult.*

DISCOVERING NORTH AMERICA

According to the traditions of the Chumash Indians, the world was divided into three layers. The top layer was inhabited by powerful supernatural beings, such as Moon, Morning Star, and Sun and his daughters, who lived in a crystal house. The middle layer was home to humans and was separated from the upper world by a giant eagle, who supported the heavens with his great wings. On the bottom layer lived dangerous creatures called *nunashish*. At night, they often crept into the middle world to frighten or harm its inhabitants.

When the earth was created, some of the supernatural beings, known as First People, lived in the middle world and acted just as humans do. But then a great flood came, and most of the First People were turned into the animals, plants, and natural forces, such as thunder, that are now found on the earth. The remaining First People went to live in the upper world and became Sky People. One of these beings, Snilemun, or Coyote of the Sky, created humans to live in the middle layer. Thereafter, Snilemun watched over the Chumash to ensure that they and the rest of the middle world's inhabitants were well.

Up until the late 18th century, when Europeans arrived on the west coast of North America, the Chumash Indians controlled a vast region in southwestern California that included large portions of present-day Los Angeles, Ventura, Santa Barbara, and San Luis Obispo counties as well as the islands of San Miguel, Santa Rosa, Santa Cruz, and Anacapa. Chumash society was a complex system of interrelated villages. These settlements were part of a huge trade network that included many different Indian groups and covered much of the west coast of the United States.

Archaeologists (scholars who study the remains of past societies) are not certain when the ancestors of the Chumash first arrived in southwestern California, but it is possible that they began to settle there sometime between 12,000 and 27,000 years ago. Scientists theorize that the early pioneers, whom they call Paleo-Indians, slowly migrated across a strip of land from Siberia to Alaska. This land bridge (named Beringia after the Bering Strait, which now covers it) came into existence during the Ice Age. At this time, the average temperature of the earth was a great deal cooler, and much of the water in the ocean froze, causing the sea level to drop. As a result, the shallowest portions of the sea floor, such as the strip between Asia and North America, were exposed.

When the first groups of Paleo-Indians arrived in North America, they did not know that they had reached a new continent. They were simply following herds of big game as they had done in Asia. Within a few generations, however, these Indians had settled in virtually every inhabitable part of North and South America, including the area that became the homeland of the Chumash in southwestern California.

It is difficult for scholars to reconstruct the way of life of the Paleo-Indians because wind, rain, and soil erosion have destroyed or buried many places where they may have lived. Only

a few of their tools have been found along with the bones of some of the animals that they hunted, such as giant ground sloths, mammoths, camels, and bison. Archaeologists believe that these Indians probably lived in small bands of closely related individuals. Such groups most likely lived in a series of temporary camps, which they established in various areas of their territory during different seasons of the year. In this way, they could have hunted and gathered the resources that were available in those areas and at those times. However, almost every aspect of scholars' reconstructions of these early peoples' culture is based on conjecture.

The earliest evidence of settled Indian villages in southwestern California dates to about 10,000 years ago. These archaeological sites, which scholars classify as belonging to the Early Period of Chumash culture, consist of the remains of villages and camps and were probably inhabited by ancestors of the Chumash. Most sites in these earliest times were located along creeks or streams, often near the seashore and often in places that offered a good view of surrounding areas. These places contain evidence of a well-adapted culture relying on both land and ocean resources.

These Early Period villages were usually small, consisting of between 3 and 10 houses and containing from 10 to 60 inhabitants. The villagers gathered a wide variety of plants, but grass seeds were the most common resource. The

A stone spearpoint found at Folsom, New Mexico. This style of point was made by Paleo-Indians, who were the ancestors of all Indian groups in North America.

clothes

Indians removed the seeds by hand and placed them in twined baskets. After the harvest, the Indians made flour by pouring small amounts of seeds onto large, flat milling stones and grinding them up with a small hand-held stone called a mano. Because so many of these grinding stones have been found in Early Period sites, the Indians who flourished at this time are also sometimes referred to as the Millingstone Culture.

food

The Millingstone Indians gathered many other types of food resources during the different seasons in their environment. During the winter and spring, the Indians collected bulbs, clovers, and other greens. In summer, they collected roots, grasses, and bulbs as well as the more common seed resources, and in fall and winter, they gathered several types of nuts and berries.

food

Throughout the year, the Indians hunted and fished for a variety of animals. They made the tools for hunting from the natural resources of their homeland. Spears and knives were tipped with sharpened bone and stone. Handles, clubs, and traps were commonly made of wood. Fishhooks, fiber fishing lines, baskets, and nets were used to catch marine resources. Fishing was either done from shore or possibly from canoes and rafts. These vessels were also used to travel to and from the Channel Islands, which were inhabited at least part of the year during the Early Period.

tools

weapons

The Millingstone Indians used animal resources to manufacture their clothing, ornaments, and other everyday items. From bone, they fashioned hair ornaments, earrings, and pendants. From hides, feathers, and sinews, they made skirts, shirts, capes, and headdresses. The Indians also used bone to manufacture flutes and whistles and used shells to make ornaments and shell-bead currency.

Archaeologists believe that during the first half of the Early Period (5,000 to 10,000 years ago), the Indians lived in an egalitarian society—one in which there were no class divisions. There was probably someone in each village who acted as the spokesperson or chief, but this person (most likely a man) was chosen because of his attributes, not because of his class position. In order to become chief, a person had to possess honesty, strength, skill at hunting and fishing, and skill at negotiating with villagers and with leaders of other villages. Because these abilities required a great deal of learning, chiefs probably had to be between 30 and 50 years of age.

Each village was an autonomous unit. The villagers collected from the territory surrounding them the food and other resources that they needed. However, in the event of a poor harvest or a drought, the leader of a village might request permission to collect food in the territory of an adjoining settlement. Villages also practiced a number of ceremonies, usually on their own but occasionally at gatherings of several communities. These large gatherings were organized by the chiefs or village

ROUTE OF PALEO-INDIANS ACROSS THE BERING LAND BRIDGE

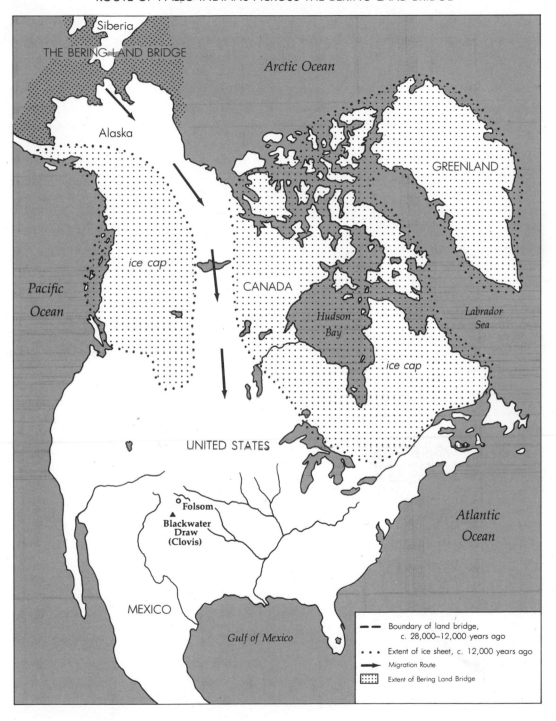

Siberia

THE BERING LAND BRIDGE

Arctic Ocean

Alaska

GREENLAND

ice cap

Pacific
Ocean

CANADA

Hudson
Bay

Labrador
Sea

ice cap

UNITED STATES

Atlantic
Ocean

Folsom

Blackwater
Draw
(Clovis)

MEXICO

Gulf of Mexico

– – Boundary of land bridge,
c. 28,000–12,000 years ago

• • • Extent of ice sheet, c. 12,000 years ago

→ Migration Route

▦ Extent of Bering Land Bridge

leaders of the various villages. The group would decide on such conditions as the location and timing of the festivals, the items necessary for the performance of rituals, and the types of sacred dances that were to be performed.

The way of life of the early Millingstone people seems to have been a successful one. Archaeologists continue to find evidence that around 5,000 years ago villages began to increase in size and population. It is also probable that at this time new villages began to appear as the result of the splitting up of large villages. During this period, the climate of the region also began to become drier, causing the environment and consequently the Indians' food resources to alter.

Archaeological investigation of these later sites has shown that the social organization of the Millingstone Indians began to change as well. As villages became larger, the inhabitants began to have control over larger resource areas and to accumulate more goods. This in turn created a more powerful position for the village chiefs. Leaders began to pass down their wealth and knowledge, and eventually their position, within their family.

Chiefs continued to handle the political relations between villages and these became more involved as well. During the latter half of the Millingstone Period, villages began to harvest resources collectively. In a departure from the past, however, the chiefs would take control of the food and tool materials and then redistribute them among the villages according to need. This cooperation between villages was especially helpful during catastrophes, such as famines or storms, because it provided a stored-up source of food resources to the needy.

During the second half of the Early Period, the Indians continued to use many of the same types of foods as they had in the past. However, there were some significant changes. For example, new types of seeds, nuts, and berries were harvested and ground on a new type of milling stone. These new tools were much bigger and heavier than their predecessors and were used with several different types of manos, the choice of which depended on the item that was being processed.

Among the most important new resources that the Indians began to use were acorns, which they collected from the huge oak forests in their territory. These forests began to replace earlier types of foliage when the climate change occurred. This new food source required a processing technology other than the milling stone and mano method. In order to turn acorns into flour, the Indians placed the nuts in stone mortars, or bowls, and then pounded them with long, cylindrical pestles, or pounding staffs. Acorns, which were not used at all during the first half of the Early Period, soon became the most important food in the daily life of the Indians. Indeed, ground acorn meal was probably consumed almost every day for the several thousand years before the arrival of Europeans.

Some things did not change in the Indians' daily life, however. They continued to make and use the same kinds of traps, weapons, and fishing equipment, although they also began to use canoes more often for fishing and for hunting marine mammals. The Indians still made shell and bone ornaments and instruments, performed ceremonies, and engaged in the same everyday activities that they had in the past.

Throughout the Early Period, villages continued to increase in size and complexity and the social practices of the people continued to change. About 3,000 years ago, the way of life of these Indians came to closely resemble the Chumash world described by the Spanish in the 16th and 17th centuries. ▲

Rafael Solares making stone projectile points, photographed in the
late 19th century. Solares was an invaluable source of information
on traditional Chumash culture during Leon de Cessac's work in the
region. Unfortunately, the ancient Chumash objects that Cessac discovered and excavated now reside in the Musée de l'Homme (Museum of Mankind) in Paris, France—far from the descendants of the
people who made them.

A HOMELAND
OF
ABUNDANCE

Region

The area that made up the traditional Chumash homeland has a rich and varied environment. It consists of a strip of land along the central and southern coast of California and measures approximately 250 miles long and 50 to 75 miles wide. There are many separate microenvironments in the region, each having its own climate, plant groups, animal species, and geologic features. Along the coastal areas, there are many sheltered lagoons and sandy beaches as well as rocky shorelines exposed to large waves. Farther inland, flat terraces, separated from one another by small streams, stretch eastward toward gently rolling hills and valleys. At the easternmost border of the Chumash homeland, the hills grade into steep, rugged mountains that attain heights of up to 5,000 feet. The islands of the Chu-

mash territory, which range from 12 to 30 miles from the mainland, are rugged, and for this reason most settlement of the islands was restricted to the coastal portions. Santa Cruz, Santa Rosa, and San Miguel islands were inhabited year-round. Anacapa Island, however, has no permanent source of fresh water and was therefore inhabited seasonally.

The climate of southern California is characterized by a dry summer and mild winter and has a considerable amount of sunshine throughout the year (there are generally only 10 to 15 inches of rain per year). The coastal areas experience temperatures that vary between 50 to 70 degrees Fahrenheit. Inland, the temperatures are more extreme, sometimes reaching as low as 30 degrees in the winter and as high as 100 degrees in the summer. Weather conditions on the islands are similar to those on the coast, although the islands tend to receive less rain and are exposed to violent windstorms, particularly during the winter.

The homeland of the Chumash was rich in resources, and the Indians took full advantage of it. The Chumash made large domed houses from the trees and plants in their territory. Each dwelling, which was between 15 and 50 feet in diameter and 5 to 15 feet tall, consisted of a framework of willow poles that were first stripped of bark and then driven several inches into the ground. The tops of the poles were then bent in toward one another and joined together to form a dome-shaped shell. Some larger houses also had a central pole that supported the roof. In order to form the walls, smaller poles were interwoven horizontally among the uprights and then tied with strips of bark to keep them in place. After the frame was prepared, mats made from twined tule, or bulrushes, were placed over it and tied to the frame in a pattern similar to the shingles on a modern-day house. This made the structure almost waterproof. Each dwelling was equipped with two openings—one in the top that allowed smoke to escape and one on the side that served as a doorway. Inside the structure, the Chumash built a small central fire and placed sleeping mats around the side.

The Chumash used plant fiber to make baskets in a wide variety of sizes and shapes. These served many pur-poses, including the storage of foods and other materials and the processing and the collecting of food. They were so skilled that they could take dried grasses and willow twigs and weave a basket that was watertight. They also wove together different colored fibers to create intricate and beautiful patterns in their baskets. Today, the Chumash are highly regarded as among the finest basket makers in the world.

From wood they fashioned such things as knife handles, bowls, bows, arrow shafts, and needles. They also used wood to make several different types of canoes for fishing and transportation on the ocean and lagoons. The dugout was made from the trunk of a large tree, usually between 15 and 30 feet long. The Chumash placed hot rocks along one side of the tree to burn and soften the wood. They then carved out the burned sections and finished shaping the boat with stone or bone carving tools.

Another type of canoe that the Chumash made was the balsa. In order to make this boat, they cut stalks of tule into six-foot lengths and allowed them to dry. The Indians then bundled the stalks and tied them together to form a 10-to-15-foot canoe. These vessels held only a few people and were probably used for short trips because they were not very durable.

The most unique Chumash canoe was the *tomol*, or plank canoe, which sometimes took up to six months to create. In order to build a tomol, a canoe

The intricate decoration on these 18th- and 19th-century Chumash baskets and trays was created by interweaving dyed black twine among the natural fibers. The large tray in the back is not of a traditional style and was probably introduced during the Spanish mission period.

maker first cut several small, flat boards by splitting pieces of driftwood that he had gathered from the beach. Then he used bone and stone tools to shape the split pieces into rectangular boards about three-quarters of an inch thick. Finally, he made them smooth by rubbing them with a piece of sharkskin. Once all the pieces were ready, the canoe maker made small holes in the sides of the planks, using a stone drill. He then used fiber string to sew the pieces together end to end and sealed the holes and the cracks between the boards with tar. Occasionally, a canoe maker painted a tomol red and decorated it with shells.

Tomols were usually about 30 feet long and could carry about 4,000 pounds. They were most often used for trips between the islands and the mainland Chumash settlements. The canoes usually carried 6 people but could hold up to 12 people. Using double-sided paddles, rowers could propel a tomol as fast as a person could run. Possession of a tomol was a sign of high position in Chumash society, and only the members of the upper classes were allowed to own them.

Stone was another resource of great importance to the Chumash. Certain types of stone were chosen for specific tasks, based on the particular properties that they possessed. For instance, dense, round stones were for cooking because they retained heat well. The Chumash would heat rocks and use them to line their hearths and ovens.

Or they would place the stones in a fire until they became hot and then transfer the stones with tongs to baskets or stone bowls filled with water and food. The hot rocks would quickly bring to a boil such things as mush, soup, or stew.

From other types of stone, the Chumash made milling stones, manos, and bowls by pecking and grinding them into the desired shape with harder stones. They made scrapers, knives, and arrow points by chipping or flaking off pieces from a glassy core stone until it was properly shaped and sharpened. A toolmaker would strike the edge of the core with a hammer of stone or bone, causing small flakes or chips to fall off. In this way, a very sharp cutting edge was produced.

The Chumash used soft, brightly colored rocks for making paints. Such rocks were easily ground into fine powders and when mixed with a liquid created different pigments, including red, yellow, blue, and green. The Chumash used these colors to paint their body during dances, to color wooden items such as bowls and canoes, and to create pictures on rock walls.

The Chumash also used a resource called asphaltum, a naturally occurring, gluey tar. They employed it to mend broken bowls, to seal the cracks in canoes, to attach stone points to wooden handles, to mount shell beads, and even to trade for other items with neighboring tribes. Asphaltum was greatly sought after because it could be used to waterproof objects. For example, to make a basket water-resistant, the Chumash placed small lumps of asphaltum into a newly made basket. Then they dropped small heated rocks into the basket and rolled them around in circles. Soon the rocks melted the tar and coated the inside of the basket with it. After the tar dried, the baskets could be used for storing water.

The Chumash people relied on plants more than on any other single item in their territory. In fact, three-quarters of their diet consisted of plant foods. Therefore, they made it their business to learn everything they could about each plant's life cycle, growing season, and rate of productivity. In this way, the Chumash could plan their

Beads (left and right), an awl (bottom), and a hair ornament (top) made from bone and decorated with inlaid shell beads. In order to attach the beads to the objects, the Chumash embedded them in asphaltum, a tar that occurred naturally in Chumash territory.

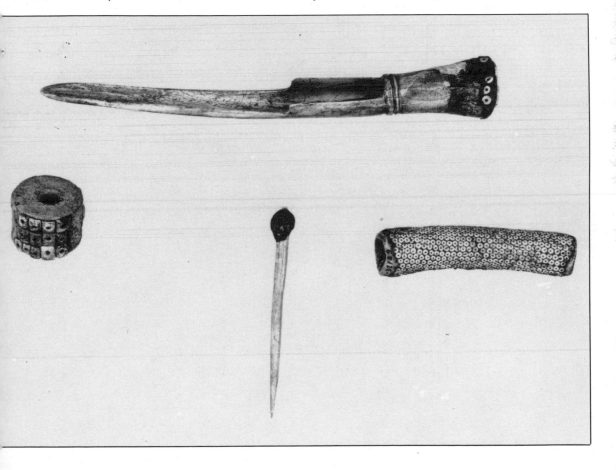

A museum diorama of a group of Chumash Indians returning home after a food-gathering and fishing expedition.

A mission-era Chumash basket, decorated with figures of animals and cacti. This style of basket was probably used for winnowing, or separating, seeds from their husk after they had been
pounded.

food-gathering expeditions with these factors in mind.

The Chumash used many different parts of the plants they gathered, including the flowers, leaves, seeds, roots, and bulbs. Each of these different plant resources was available at a different season of the year. For example, the Chumash harvested fresh leaves and underground bulbs and roots during the rainy season in winter and early spring, when these plants first sprouted new growth. Winter was also the time when the Chumash gathered fresh clovers, mustard greens, and other herbs.

The rainy season ended in April, and the plants that blossomed in warmer, drier weather began to produce flowers and seeds. The Chumash gathered these resources, such as red maids and chia, in the middle of spring. Plants with smaller seeds that grew on slopes or flat areas were harvested until June, when the summer dry season began.

At the onset of the dry season, large plants with deep roots began to produce fruits, such as manzanita berries, which the Chumash gathered. During this time, the Chumash also burned off the dead plant stems in their food-gathering areas. The Indians regulated the fires so that they would burn quickly, in order to prevent damage to larger vegetation and trees. In this way, the Chumash reduced dead leaves, twigs, and other brush to ashes, which fertilized the bulbs, clover, and other herbs that sprouted during the winter season.

Fall was a time for gathering ripe nuts and berries from the large trees and bushes; the harvest included acorns, pine nuts, wild strawberries, laurel berries, madrona berries, and cattail seeds. One particularly interesting bulb used by the Chumash was soaproot, which the Indians identified by the brown tufts of its leaves. Chumash women would dig up the root with a digging stick and then pry it out of the ground. Then they would remove the foliage, leaving a two-to-three-inch-long potatolike bulb. The plant could then be prepared in diverse ways.

If the soaproot was pounded fresh and sprinkled into still water, it would paralyze the gills of fish. The fish would then float to the surface, and the Chumash could easily collect them. If it was allowed to dry slightly, soaproot formed a resinous material that was used to coat tool handles and brushes in order to make them last longer. The freshly ground pulp could also be used as a soap for washing hair, skin, and clothing. Most remarkably, if the fresh bulb was placed in a rock-lined oven and baked for half a day, it became a tasty and nutritious food.

Of all the resources that the Chumash gathered, the most important was the acorn. This nut was found in vast numbers in the oak forests of Chumash territory. In order to gather as many acorns as possible, hundreds of men, women, and children from several villages would work together to collect these nutritious seeds. In comparison, most plant-gathering expeditions consisted of individuals or small groups of people.

Food plants were processed in a wide variety of ways. Bulbs, mushrooms, and fresh clover were simply picked and eaten without any preparation. Other foods were steamed or boiled in order to make them edible or to enhance their flavor. Seeds were eaten raw, toasted among hot coals, or ground into flour. This flour was then added to water or soup to form the basis of a mush or porridge. Occasionally the seed flour was fried or baked into cakes and flavored with different types of spices or vegetables. The roots of plants such as the yucca were baked in large ovens for as long as 24 hours before they could be eaten. They too were either consumed immediately or ground into flour and made into cakes for long-term storage.

Because the Indians relied heavily on acorns for food, the Chumash women invented a special means of preparing them for consumption. The process was similar to the mano and milling stone method used by the Chumash's ancestors. The Chumash method, however, employed a stone mortar and pestle. A Chumash woman preparing to mash acorns would first fashion a mortar, or container for grinding, from a large, squarish rock on top of which she fastened a bottomless basket with tar glue. She then placed handfuls of acorns into the basket and pounded them with a pestle (a long, cylindrical rock).

Although pounded into a flour, the acorns were still not edible. Most acorns contain a bitter chemical, known as tannic acid, that must be removed from the flour before it can be eaten. Chumash women did this by lining a basket or a shallow basin with leaves, placing the flour in it, and then slowly pouring water over the top of the flour until it was completely covered. The water would slowly leach through the flour, carrying the tannic acid with it. Chumash women had to repeat this process four or five times if the acorns were particularly bitter. Once all the preparation was completed, the flour was used to make mush or was baked in the form of cakes, which were flavored with a variety of spices, meats, and berries.

The foods that the Chumash did not eat immediately were kept for future use. For example, every Chumash house had one or more large basketry granaries, the largest of which could hold as much as 1,000 pounds of acorns. These granaries were usually made of woven willow twigs and placed on stilts to keep them off the ground. The acorns held in the granaries would be used by the village inhabitants almost every day.

In addition to being used for food, a large number of plants were used to make medicines to treat a wide variety of illnesses and ailments, including stomachaches, headaches, colds, infections, and broken bones. Plants were also regularly placed in graves with corpses and used in religious ceremonies. For example, sage leaves mixed

A carved oak bowl made during the mission era and decorated around the rim with shell-bead inlay. Few of these finely crafted objects, used for serving food, survive today.

with water were used to purify musical instruments before dances, and tobacco was smoked in stone pipes during sweatlodge rituals.

Although meat made up only a small portion of the Chumash's diet, they hunted a wide variety of animals. The most common animals hunted were elks, antelope, and especially deer. In order to hunt deer, Chumash hunters camouflaged themselves by wearing the skin and horns of a deer as a headdress. W' :n they spotted a deer in the forest, they approached it while making movements that imitated those of the animal. If a hunter was able to

continued on page 36

CHUMASH MYTHOLOGY

The Chumash, like all other peoples, developed an elaborate mythology that gave meaning to the objects and events in their world. The Indians used these myths to explain the existence of natural elements (such as rain and thunder), to illustrate proper behavior, and to make sense of the human life cycle. Just as the Bible serves to guide and teach Jews and Christians about the world and its creation, the mythology of the Chumash helped them maintain what they considered full and proper lives.

During the mission era, much of Chumash culture was lost or deliberately destroyed, but some aspects have survived, including the Indians' oral history. The major forces in its preservation were anthropologist John P. Harrington and a group of six Chumash elders, who in 1912 embarked on a decade-long project during which they recorded many of the Chumash's myths. The project eventually produced several thousand pages of notes that today stand as a testimony to the rich religious and cultural traditions of the Chumash Indians.

The following myth tells the story of the journey that a person's soul takes after death. It was told to Harrington by Ynezeño Chumash María Solares, who was born at Mission Santa Ynéz during the first half of the 19th century.

Three days after a person has been buried the soul comes up out of the grave in the evening. Between the third and fifth day it wanders about the world visiting the places it used to frequent in life. On the fifth day after death the soul returns to the grave to oversee the destruction of its property before leaving for Šimilaqša [the Land of the Dead across the Sea]. The soul goes first to Point Conception, which is a wild and stormy place. It was called humqaq, and there was no village there. In ancient times no one ever went near humqaq. They only went near there to make sacrifices at a great šawil [shrine]. There is a place at humqaq below the cliff that can only be reached by rope, and there is a pool of water there like a basin, into which fresh water continually drips. And there in the stone can be seen the footprints of women and children. There the spirit of the dead bathes and paints itself. Then it sees a light to the westward and goes toward it through the air, and thus reaches the land of Šimilaqša.

Sometimes in the evening people at La Quemada village would see a soul passing by on its way to Point Conception. Sometimes these were the souls of people who had died, but sometimes they were souls that had temporarily left the body. The people of La Quemada would motion with their hands at the soul and tell it to return, to go back east, and they would clap their hands. Sometimes the soul would respond and turn back, but other times it would simply swerve a little from its course and continue

María Solares, photographed in 1916. Solares was probably anthropologist John P. Harrington's most knowledgeable informant on Chumash mythology.

on to Šimilaqša. When the people of La Quemada saw the soul it shone like a light, and it left a blue trail behind it. The disease from which the person had died was seen as a fiery ball at its side. When the soul turned back, as it sometimes did, anyone at La Quemada who might have recognized it would hurry to the village where the man whose soul it was lived, and if the sick man then drank a lot of toloache [a drink made from the jimsonweed] he might recover and not die. [Sometimes] a short time after the soul passed La Quemada the people there would hear a report like a distant cannon shot, and know that was the sound of the closing of the gate of Šimilaqša as the soul entered.

The old people said that there were three lands in the world to the west: wit, ʔayaya, and Šimilaqša. These were somewhat like purgatory, hell, and heaven. When the soul leaves Point Conception and crosses the sea, it first reaches the Land of Widows. When the women there get old their friends dip them in a spring and when they awake they are young again. And they never eat, though they have all kinds of food there. They merely take a handful of food and smell it and throw it away, and as soon as they do so it turns to feces. And when they are thirsty they just smell the water and their thirst is quenched. Once past the Land of Widows the soul comes to a deep ravine through which it must pass. The road is all cut up and consists of deep, fine earth as a result of so many souls passing over it. In the ravine are two huge stones that continually part and clash together, part and clash together, so that any person who got caught between them would be crushed. Any living person who attempted to pass would be killed, but souls pass through unharmed.

Once past the clashing rocks the soul comes to a place where there are two gigantic qaq [ravens] perched on each side of the trail, and who each peck out an eye as the soul goes by. But there are many poppies growing there in the ravine and the soul quickly picks two of these and inserts them in each eye-socket and so is able to see again immediately. When the soul finally gets to Šimilaqša it is given eyes made of blue abalone. After leaving the ravine the soul comes to La Tonadora, the woman who stings with her tail. She kills any living person who comes by, but merely annoys the soul who passes safely.

Just beyond this woman lies a body of water that separates this world from the next, with a bridge that the soul must cross to reach Šimilaqša. The souls of murderers and poisoners and other evil people never reach the bridge, but are turned to stone from the neck down. They remain there on the near shore forever, moving their eyes and watching other souls pass. When the pole begins to fall the soul starts quickly across, but when it reaches the middle two huge monsters rise from the water on either side and give a loud cry, attempting to frighten it so that it falls into the water. If the soul belongs to someone who had no ʔatišwɨn [spirit helper] or who did not know about the old religion and did not drink toloache—someone who merely lived in ignorance—it falls into the water and the lower part of the body changes to that of a frog, turtle, snake, or fish. The water is full of these beings, who are thus

Fernando Librado, here shown stringing shell beads, provided Harrington with information on the Chumash's traditional political organization and rituals.

undergoing punishment. When they are hungry they crawl out of the water and wander through the hills nearby looking for cacomites [edible bulbs] to eat. The old people used to say that someone who drank toloache always passed the pole safely for they were strong of spirit.

Once the soul has crossed the bridge it is safe in Šimilaqša. There are two roads leading from the bridge—one goes straight ahead and the other goes to the left. . . . Souls live in Šimilaqša forever and never get old. It is packed full of souls. They harvest islay, sweet islay, and there is no end of it. Every kind of food is there in abundance. When children die they take the same route as adults. The qaq peck out their eyes, but they have no other troubles on the journey. They pass the bridge easily, for the monsters that try to frighten other souls do not appear.

continued from page 31

come close to the deer, he used a stone-tipped spear. From a greater distance, the hunter would shoot the deer using a bow and arrow.

Bows, which were not commonly used until about A.D. 500, were usually made from a piece of hard wood that had been bent, heated, scraped, and shaped into the proper form. The bowstring was made from either *tok* (milkweed fiber) or animal tendons. The Chumash made several types of arrows—some made from solid wood, some made of hollow cane, and others having a solid shaft with a small stone point. The arrow makers used bird feathers to make the arrow stable in flight.

Rabbits and squirrels were also commonly hunted by the Chumash. They killed these animals by using bows and arrows, throwing clubs, throwing sticks, or using slingshots. Sometimes the hunters placed long nets along the ground. Then they formed a long line and moved toward the net, driving the animals into it. The Chumash also used pointed sticks to dig up the underground burrows and nests of animals, such as rabbits, squirrels, gophers, and mice.

The Chumash used many kinds of traps and snares to capture animals. The simplest was a long string with a loop at one end. A hunter would place the snare on a trail and then hide until a rabbit or some other animal passed by. If an animal stepped into the loop, the hunter would quickly jerk the string

and capture it. Sometimes a hunter would attach the looped string to a bent bush or tree branch that would spring up when an animal stepped in the loop. Another technique was to hold a log or rock up with a small stick. A hunter then placed food under the rock and pulled the stick out by a string when an animal started to eat.

The Chumash hunted a number of smaller animals for food, such as turtles, frogs, and various kinds of lizards and snakes. They also hunted several fur-bearing animals for their skin, teeth, and claws. These included coyotes, gray foxes, badgers, skunks, mountain lions, and bobcats. It is possible that they also hunted bears.

When hunting birds, the Chumash used arrows, nets, clubs, and slingshots. If they were trying to capture waterfowl, such as ducks and geese, the Chumash used decoys that resembled the birds. The decoys attracted the birds to an area where the Chumash could easily throw nets over them. No matter what type of animal was killed, the hunter would always say a special prayer to thank the animal's spirit for providing him with food and other resources.

Having lived along the Pacific Ocean for more than 9,000 years, the Chumash acquired a detailed knowledge of the ocean, its inhabitants, and their life cycles. They invented many different tools to exploit the ocean's resources. The ancestors of the Chumash fished with a small piece of bone (about

TRADITIONAL HOMELANDS OF CHUMASH GROUPS

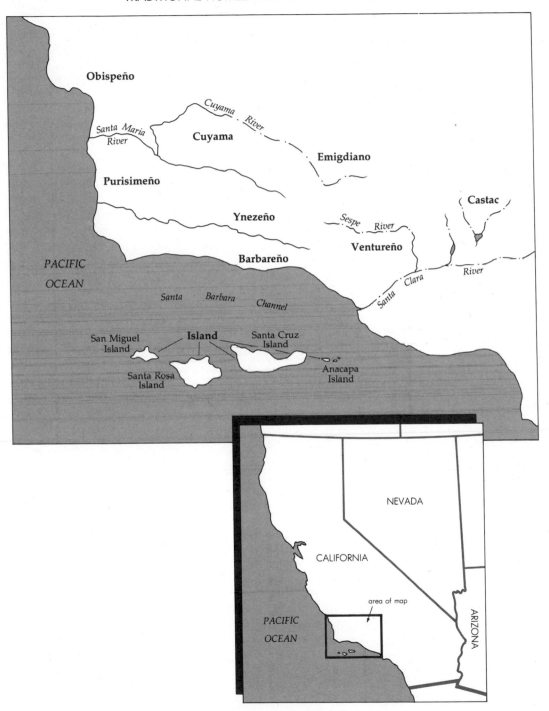

one inch long) that was pointed at each end. The barb was attached to a fiber string with tar and then baited and cast out either from the shore or from a raft. The earliest Chumash groups probably used this method of fishing as well.

About 2,500 years ago, the Chumash began to use J fishhooks for the first time. These were usually made from abalone or mussel shell that had been broken into several pieces. The sections were then shaped with a rock into an approximately circular shape, several inches in diameter. The hook maker drilled a hole in the center, enlarged it, and broke open one side of the shell to form a hook. It was most commonly baited with pieces of cactus or very small fish and used in shallow water.

The Chumash made another type of fishhook that was used to catch tuna and other fish that swam in groups. It was dragged behind a boat through schools of these fish. Fishline was made from the fibers of either yucca or milkweed.

The Chumash also made nets from this material and cast them into the surf. After hauling the nets in, they collected the fish that had been trapped. Sometimes they dragged nets behind canoes in order to catch fish. They also used small basketry traps that were baited with cactus or other bait and weighted with rocks. The traps were pulled up when fish swam into them to eat the bait.

The Chumash hunted several types of marine mammals. On land, the Indians killed seals, sea lions, and otters when these animals were sunning themselves on rocks or on the shore. Hunters would creep up on the animals and kill them with spears or clubs. In the water, the Chumash harpooned animals, such as dolphins, from canoes with wooden spears that were tipped with bone or stone points.

Archaeologists have also found remains of the California gray whale at Chumash sites. They do not believe, however, that the Indians hunted these animals. Scholars think that the Chumash waited until a whale was stranded on shore and then butchered it for its meat, bones, and other useful parts.

The Chumash collected several dozen different types of shellfish, but the most common were abalones, mussels, and clams. The Chumash gathered mussels and abalones on the rocky parts of the coast. Along the flat, sandy beaches and shallow bays, they dug up clams that were burrowed in the soft sand.

Shellfish were prepared in a variety of ways. Although they were most often simply eaten raw, when the Chumash cooked them, they usually steamed, boiled, or roasted them in hearths or ovens. In order to do this, the Indians would dig a basin in the sand one or two feet deep and line it with large rocks. Driftwood and other brush were used to build a fire and heat the rocks. The Indians would then put down a layer of seaweed and place various shellfish on top of it. Next, they spread another layer of seaweed over the top of the foods and finally covered the pit with sand in order to contain the heat. The food was then allowed to cook for up to half a day.

The Chumash lacked nothing in their resource-rich environment. They were even able to build up surpluses of foods, tools, and raw materials that gave them a position of great power in the trading network of the region. In order to control and conduct these business transactions, the Chumash developed a complex political structure that enabled many members of the nation to amass great wealth. The Chumash's prestigious position remained unthreatened until the arrival of Europeans. ▲

Chumash Indian José Peregrino Romero was born in the mid-19th century on Santa Cruz Island but spent most of his childhood in Ventura. He served as a research consultant to ethnographer John P. Harrington during his research among the Chumash in the 1920s and 1930s.

A THRIVING
WAY OF LIFE

When the first Spanish explorers landed among the Chumash, they found a very complex and diverse culture. In the early 16th century, the nation consisted of some 20,000 to 30,000 people who inhabited from 75 to 100 villages. Some towns were home to only a few single-family dwellings, whereas others held more than 1,000 people. The Spanish explorers described the Chumash as attractive, strong, graceful, inventive, and industrious. They noted that the men were between five and six feet tall and the women about four and a half to five feet tall. Their health was generally good, and some appeared to be well over 70 years old.

The majority of Chumash men wore little clothing, usually only a hide or fiber loincloth, although they occasion-ally added a cape of deerskin or some other hide. They adorned themselves with necklaces and woven belts and placed pins and knives in their hair for decoration. Poor members of the society wore loincloths made from grass or shredded bark, whereas wealthy Chumash men dressed in capes of otter, seal, or other fur.

Women's clothing consisted of skirts of deer or rabbit skin that were embellished along the bottom with shells and other ornaments. On their upper body, they wore shirts or capes made from fox, rabbit, deer, or sea otter skin. Poor women used soft grasses to make their skirts and stuck pieces of tar to the hem in order to keep the grasses weighted down. Chumash women adorned themselves with shell- and seed-bead necklaces and earrings, and they wore decorative pins in their hair. They pierced their ears and wore earrings of stone and bone. Both sexes made extensive use of body paints, with red and black the preferred colors.

There were many different types of Chumash settlements. Each village was connected to all the others through social, political, and economic ties. These villages, which the Spanish called *ranch-*erías, were arranged in provinces or districts. The districts were organized into three large regional divisions—island villages, coastal villages, and interior villages. Scholars have divided the Chumash into nine subgroups—Obispeño, Purisimeño, Cuyama, Ynezeño, Barbareño, Emigdiano, Castac, Ventureño, and Island. All spoke one of six languages in the Chumashan branch of

Chumash abalone-shell ornaments and implements. The blades at the bottom center were used as ceremonial scratching sticks by Chumash women during their menstrual cycle. Throughout that time, girls were forbidden to touch themselves with their hands.

the Hokan language family, and all belonged to the Chumash nation.

The name Chumash was not used by the Indians to refer to themselves. "Chumash" was mistakenly used by the Spanish to describe all of the subgroups, but it is actually a mispronunciation of the name used by coastal groups to refer to the Indians on either Santa Cruz Island (*mitcúmac*), or Santa Rosa Island (*tcúmac*). It probably meant "those who make shell beads" from the Barbareño word *alchum*, meaning "money" (shell beads, the currency of the Chumash nation, were manufactured by the Island Indians). Unfortunately, there is no record of what the Chumash called themselves before the Spanish arrived.

Each regional Chumash group had special resources that were collected and processed by the inhabitants and then traded to villagers from adjacent regions. For example, island villages did not have many plant resources, but they were rich in ocean resources, such as fish, marine mammals, and shellfish, in addition to olivella shells, which the Chumash manufactured into shell-bead currency. The Island Chumash traded these shells and other items to the groups on the mainland for meats, hides, grains, and fruits. Although coastal mainland villages had the greatest number of resources, they lacked among other items some types of special stone. Therefore, they traded seafood and beads with the inland groups, who had access to large amounts of acorns and deer. During regularly held fairs, traders from villages all over the Chumash nation could make direct exchanges with one another.

This extensive trade network was active for thousands of years, and during their history, the Chumash developed an economy based on specialization. Aside from the usual political, religious, and medicinal specialists, the Chumash had craftspeople who made items as diverse as beads, headdresses, tobacco, nets, baskets, leather, tools, utensils, and canoes. Others specialized in the hunting of land mammals or in fishing. Craftspeople were organized into guilds that regulated the prices of items and access to them. For example, only the wealthiest members of Chumash society possessed the special tomols. The Spanish were so impressed by the complexity of the Chumash economy that they compared them to the Chinese, who had a powerful and thriving empire.

Along with the widespread emphasis on specialization, the Chumash developed an economy based on the use of currency, a practice uncommon in many Indian societies. The standard unit of value in the Chumash nation was a string of small white shell beads that could be wrapped around the hand once. This monetary system was first implemented by the Chumash approximately 1,000 years ago and continued until the time that the Spanish began to settle in the Indians' homeland.

The manufacture of this form of currency was an involved process. Only one type of shell, the purple olivella, could be used. It was first collected from sandy beaches of both the mainland and the Channel Islands. Each shell was struck with a rock to break it into several pieces. The usable pieces were then chipped until they were approximately circular. Next, they were placed in a tar-coated basket filled with hot coals. The pieces were then stirred into the coals, bleaching them white. The shell pieces were placed in small receptacles that had been cut into a board, and each piece was drilled through the center by means of a slender stick with a stone or bone needle inserted into one end. After the beads were drilled, they were placed on a string and ground back and forth on a flat sandstone rock until they were of the desired diameter. The more time that a bead maker spent grinding a bead, the more valuable it was considered to be.

The bustling economy of the Chumash nation attracted traders from other tribes. By trading with these people, the Chumash were able to obtain items that were not available in their territory. From the neighboring Gabrielino Indians of Santa Catalina Island, for example, the Chumash obtained steatite, a stone from which they made bowls, animal effigies, and other items. From tribes living farther away (sometimes up to 400 miles), the Chumash obtained black, glassy obsidian, with which they could make extremely sharp knives and arrow points.

Within the Chumash nation, settlements varied in size and location. The most important factor that determined the location of a village was its proximity to vital resources. These included a permanent source of water, a large and reliable supply of plant and animal foods, materials for shelter, and good sources of rock for tools and wood for fuel. It was also important that the area was safe from natural disasters, such as floods, and from invasion by other villages or enemy tribes.

Villages were usually located on flat ground and near a water source. Connecting all of the settlements was a series of trails and roads that also led to areas used for hunting animals, for collecting plant resources, and for traveling to and from the ocean and other bodies of water. Many of the modern highways in California follow original Chumash routes that were made over 9,000 years by the footsteps of the Indian people.

A typical Chumash village consisted of several domed houses, each with one or more granaries, a ceremonial dance ground, a field for game playing, and a village burial ground. Each settlement also had one or more sweatlodges, called *temescales* by the Spanish. Sweatlodges were used for a variety of purposes, both religious and nonreligious. They were, however, almost exclusively the domain of Chumash men.

Temescales were semisubterranean. The aboveground portion of a temescal was made from woven boughs and then covered with mud so that the heat from the central fire would not escape.

A prehistoric steatite bowl decorated with an incised diamond pattern. Steatite was a highly valued item in the Chumash trade network because it was durable and easy to work.

The entrance to the structure was located in the roof, through which a notched pole extended down to the floor. As part of their daily routine, Chumash men would climb down the pole and sit around a large fire, which caused them to sweat a great deal. They often sat around the fire and sang, wiping the sweat from their bodies with bone scrapers. After they had perspired sufficiently, the men would climb out of the sweathouse, run to the nearest stream or to the ocean, and plunge into the cold water. They believed that this act purified them mentally and physically.

Temescales were also used for special purposes. Hunters would use them to purify themselves before a hunt. They would sweat and then rub themselves with herbs and oils in order to hide their scent while tracking game.

People with aches and pains would use the temescales to ease their suffering.

The Chumash had a very complex social structure. They were not only divided into different families but were also separated into classes, craft unions, and groups of specialists, such as doctors, chiefs, and other ruling figures. However, the family remained the most basic unit in each village.

A typical Chumash household consisted of a husband and wife, their married sons and their spouses, and their unmarried sons and daughters. How-

The various resources and implements used by the Chumash to manufacture their shell-bead money. The small holes in the broken slab of rock (left) were used to hold shell beads while holes were drilled through them. The photograph also shows olivella shells (top center), stone drill bits (below shells), finished beads (bottom center), and a completed string of beads (bottom right).

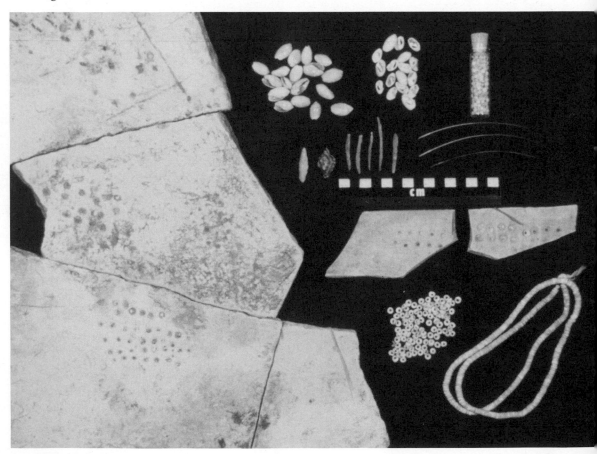

ever, a family group might also include the couples' parents, siblings, or cousins. When a man and a woman decided to marry, the prospective husband purchased his intended wife from her family with gifts such as shell beads or otter skins. The couple then moved in with the man's family.

The birthing practices of the Chumash were relatively simple. When a woman was ready to give birth, she dug a hole in the ground on the spot where she felt her first labor pain. She used heated rocks to warm the hole, lined it with straw, and awaited the birth. After the child was born, the mother cut the umbilical cord with a stone knife. She then broke the bone in the infant's nose because a flattened nose was considered a sign of beauty among the Chumash. The family asked the village shaman, or medicine man, to give the child a name. He did this according to an elaborate astrological system that was believed to ensure good luck to the child.

When a Chumash child reached puberty, she or he had to observe several ritual practices. For example, young women had to refrain from eating meat or animal fat and were forbidden to gaze directly into a fire. The most important event in the Chumash puberty rite was the ritual consumption of *toloache*, a hallucinogenic drink made from the jimsonweed. Under the guidance of a shaman, a Chumash boy or girl would drink the toloache and then fall into a dream state during which he

or she would find and acquire a spirit guide. The shaman would also interpret the adolescent's dreams as a foreshadowing of future events.

The Chumash practiced an elaborate death ritual, which was detailed in the 1775 journal of Lieutenant Pedro Fages, a Spanish official:

> When any Indian dies, they carry the body to a [ceremonial ground]. There they celebrate the mortuary ceremony, and watch all the following night[.] [S]ome of them gathered about a huge fire until daybreak; then c[a]me all the rest (men and women) and four of them beg[a]n the ceremony. One Indian smoking tobacco in a large stone pipe, goes first; he is followed by the other three, all passing [three times] around the body; but each time he passes the [corpse's] head, his companions lift the [animal] skin with which it is covered, that the priest may blow upon it three mouthfuls of smoke. On arriving at the feet, they all four together stop to sing. Then come the . . . relatives of the deceased, each one giving the chief celebrant a string of beads. Then immediately there is raised a sorrowful outcry and lamentation by all the mourners. When this sort of solemn response is ended, the four ministers take up the body, and all the Indians follow them singing to the cemetery.

Chumash cemeteries were usually located on hills or raised areas of land near the village. Placed above each grave was a marker made of wood and painted with abstract designs, and sometimes a whale rib was laid lengthwise across the grave. The Chumash also erected at the head of each grave a long pole, on which they hung a symbol of the deceased's position in the village. For example, a hunter's grave often had a bow and arrows suspended above it, and a basket maker's grave was marked with a basket.

The people of the Chumash nation all belonged to one of three classes—lower, middle, or upper. The members of the lower class did not have any skills, any family to help support them, and were lazy or criminal. The majority of the Chumash belonged to the middle class, which included hunters, food preparers, and people who made tools and utensils. These people conducted most of the activities that provided the settlements with their daily needs.

The upper class was made up of many interrelated families that lived in settlements throughout Chumash territory. Most Chumash people chose a marriage partner from their own or a nearby village. However, the upper-class people in each village often chose a partner from a village up to a hundred miles away. These marriages created networks that helped to unite the entire Chumash nation.

The highest social position in a Chumash village was that of the *wot*, or chief. The title of wot was usually passed down from father to son because the Chumash had a patrilineal descent system (in which kinship is traced through the male line). However, a person who inherited the position of wot also had to be approved by the members of the village.

Some Chumash villages had several wots living in them. These were usually the capitals, or principal villages, of the provinces and districts of the Chumash nation. In these places lived most of the political, social, and religious leaders of the region. Each principal village made one of its wots the representative for the region. At regular intervals during the year, representatives from each region would meet in a national council to discuss the problems within their region and the Chumash nation as a whole.

Each Chumash wot performed many functions for his own village. For example, each village had its own specific hunting and gathering areas, and it was the wot who regulated their use. The wot could grant permission to other villages to gather or hunt in his village's territory. In cases of severe food shortages, a council of village wots would decide how resources could best be allocated to benefit people in the neediest areas. In this way, the entire Chumash nation was ensured of survival in the event of a disaster.

In most cases, the territories where necessary plants were located were owned by important individuals within a village or sometimes by an entire village, and the right to collect resources within this area was tightly controlled.

continued on page 57

A LIVING TRADITION

The Chumash Indians traditionally controlled an environment rich in natural resources. This enabled them to manufacture all of the items that they needed to perform their daily tasks, which consisted of such diverse activities as communing with the spirit world and preparing the evening meal.

It did not matter for what task the manufactured object was intended; the Chumash applied equal attention and skill to each of the items that they created, whether it was a painting or charm that was an expression of their religious beliefs or a bowl in which to store food or water.

Although the culture of the Chumash was altered forever by European customs and objects, the tribe's traditional creations remain to this day objects of interest and study. Research into the Chumash's past continues to inspire artists, anthropologists, archaeologists, and historians. Most important, however, it has inspired the Chumash of today to reconstruct and re-create the craftwork and traditions of their ancestors.

A painting by modern-day artist Russel A. Ruiz of a coastal Chumash village as it would have looked in the late 16th century. A Spanish sailing vessel is anchored offshore in the background.

In the foreground of this Ruiz painting, set in 1795, four Chumash men paddle a tomol, or plank canoe, a type of boat unique to the Chumash. On the mainland are a Chumash village and, behind it, the buildings of Mission Santa Bárbara. In the background, a brush fire rages across the hills.

The chapel of Cieneguitas and the Chumash village of Kaswa, painted in the 1930s by Henry S. Ford. The settlement was established as a satellite of Mission Santa Bárbara so that the mission system could control a wider area of Chumash territory.

A series of Chumash rock paintings found in the hills of the tribe's southern California homeland. These works of art were expressions of Chumash religious beliefs and may have been made by shamans or other powerful people as acts of communion with the spirit world.

Reconstructed fragments of several bowls made from serpentine. The large bowl in the rear was apparently broken by its Chumash owner, who repaired it by drilling holes along the broken edges and then sewing them together with leather strips.

A storage bowl and a traditional frying pan, both made from steatite.

The bottom of a broken steatite bowl in which the Chumash mixed asphaltum, a waterproof substance. Inside the bowl are an asphaltum cake and the stone that was used to apply it to other objects.

Two prehistoric canoe effigies made from steatite. These miniature boats were used as charms by Chumash fishermen to ensure good luck during fishing expeditions. According to Chumash elder Fernando Librado, "when a canoe charm dreamer dies, [his] effigy canoes . . . are buried with him. The little boats which are found in such a grave are no longer of value, for their owner is dead, and [only] he knew how to manipulate the charms."

continued from page 48

If one group had a bad acorn harvest, it would negotiate with groups in areas that had a plentiful supply of acorns for the right to go and collect there. The needy group would either pay money to the owners of the oak groves or agree upon some service that the grove owners could request from them at a later date. These services included hosting a fiesta or providing baskets or other items.

One of the most important functions of the wot was to make preparations—such as storing up food—for a fiesta, or festive gathering. Members from each village of the many Chumash regions would bring foods and special items from their territory to sell or trade to Chumash from other villages. At these fiestas, the people would play games, arrange marriages, tell stories, and sing traditional songs. Village leaders would discuss important national issues and announce important upcoming events.

Fiestas were managed by a ceremonial leader known as a *paxa*, who was second in power to the wot. It was the paxa's responsibility to make announcements, give speeches, direct all of the fiesta events (including the construction of the sacred dancing ground), and collect offerings and money for the wot. The paxa was also in charge of overseeing the festival's religious rites and dances, which were performed by members of the *antap* cult, a Chumash religious society.

The members of the antap had to join the cult as children, but only after their parents had paid a large sum of money to the cult leaders. Because of this large fee, only the wealthiest Chumash, including the wots and their family, could afford to become members. Once a child was accepted into the society, he or she began instruction in the sacred knowledge of the organization. This included learning to sing sacred songs, speak the society's secret language, and perform the sacred dances and other rituals at fiestas. Because all of the upper-class members of Chumash society belonged to the antap cult, it created a unifying bond among the political powers throughout the nation.

The two most important times of the year for the antap, and for the Chumash nation as a whole, were the autumn acorn harvest and the winter solstice. During these events, people from all over Chumash territory would gather in the host village to trade, play games, and gamble. Village leaders conferred with one another about the problems in their homeland. The Chumash also performed rituals and gave offerings to the two most important First People—Hutash, the earth, and Kakunupmawa, the sun. The Chumash believed that if they did not properly honor and thank these deities then they would be punished with starvation or other calamities.

These rituals required a great deal of preparation. Several days before a celebration began, the paxa and several helpers constructed a special dance enclosure on the village ceremonial

A sketch by the modern-day artist Russell A. Ruiz of a traditional Chumash village during the early mission period. In the foreground are several tomols, *or plank canoes.*

ground, which was a fenced-in, level area. The enclosure, called a *siliyik* by the Chumash, was almost completely surrounded by a high wall made from woven bulrush mats, from which banners decorated with feathers were hung. It was blocked off because only certain people were allowed to witness the special dances.

The Chumash who participated in the ritual performances were all members of the antap cult. Some of them played instruments, such as bone or wood flutes, bows, cane or bone whistles, and rattles made from split branches, shells, and deer hooves. Other members danced in highly decorated garments that consisted of woven skirts with shell-bead edging and feathered hats. Each dance honored a different deity or animal that was crucial to the Chumash's well-being or had powers to which the Indians aspired.

The Chumash played many types of games both during their festivals and for everyday entertainment. These usually helped to promote friendly interaction among people and sharpened their physical and mental skills. Some games involved members of many different villages. In one type of game, two teams raced from village to village along a main road, each team kicking a small hide-covered ball. Another popular team game was played on a field and was similar to soccer. Individuals often played hoop-and-stick, a game in which a wooden hoop was rolled along the ground and a stick or spear was thrown through it. They also participated in many types of guessing games. The Chumash often bet money or goods on the outcome of the games.

Chumash shamans were particularly busy during the festivals, but they played an important role in their village throughout the year. They were responsible for a wide variety of activities, such as interpreting dreams, naming children, reading astrological events, and forecasting or averting storms. The shaman's most important task, however, was the curing of disease, whether it was physical, mental, or spiritual.

In order to combat illness, a shaman employed a number of curing methods. For example, if a person had a pain in his or her side, the shaman might use a hollow tube to ritually suck out the sickness, or if a person had a headache, a heated curing stone (a small carved pendant usually made of steatite) would be pressed against the person's head. Chumash shamans also employed many of the plants found in their territory, including sage, willow bark, and elderberry, to relieve muscle aches, colds, and fevers.

Shamans were the intermediaries between the world of the Chumash and that of the supernatural, which was the source of power. If a person wished to acquire some of this power, which provided aid in hunting, decision making, and fighting illness, he or she needed to make contact with the world of the supernatural. To establish this contact, the person needed to participate in a secret ritual that had to be performed by a shaman. During the ceremony, the person drank toloache and entered a hallucinatory state in which he or she contacted the spirit world. There, the person could meet with his or her spirit helper, which might be anything from one of the First People to an ordinary plant. Once this relationship had been established, the person could call upon his or her spirit helper to use its special power in time of need.

The shamans themselves often had several spirit helpers and were therefore extremely powerful. As a result, they were somewhat feared as well as respected in their respective villages. The Chumash believed that power itself was neutral and that all beings, both human and supernatural, were able to use this power for either good or bad purposes. They thought that the world was kept in balance only as long as people behaved properly in daily

A diorama depicting daily life in a traditional Chumash village. In the foreground, a woman is pouring water over acorn meal in order to wash out its bitter acid, behind her a woman pounds food using a mortar and pestle, and in the background other village members engage in various activities.

life and performed ceremonies in the correct manner. According to the Chumash, everything on the earth possessed some spiritual power. Therefore, religion was a part of each daily activity, whether it was collecting seeds, finding rocks for stone tools, or performing ritual dances.

The most fascinating and beautiful expressions of Chumash religious beliefs are the colorful paintings that the Indians made on the bare rock walls in the mountains of their homeland. Rock art was usually made in remote caves and crevices that only certain people, such as shamans, were allowed to enter. Scholars theorize that these places may have been associated with the presence of First People and were therefore considered sacred locations.

The content of the paintings varies throughout the Chumash homeland, but all are stylistically similar. Design motifs include anthropomorphic, or humanlike, figures that are composites of several animal and human characteristics; figures that resemble marine mammals, fishes, and birds; and abstract figures that appear to be based on the sun and other stars, comets, meteors, and wheels. Individual depictions were often painted on top of previous works, suggesting that the sites were used over a long period of time. The strange and unearthly figures were most likely painted as part of a religious ritual.

The Chumash made their paints by grinding up various colored minerals that occurred naturally in their home-

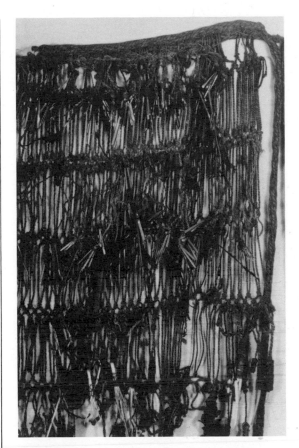

A detail of a woven fiber skirt decorated with bird feathers. This garment would have been worn by a member of the Chumash antap cult during a ritual dance.

land. From an iron ore called hematite and from cinnibar, a mercury ore, they obtained red pigment, and they ground up ash and charcoal in order to make black. Although these were the most common colors used in rock paintings, the Chumash occasionally used white, blue, green, yellow, gray, or brown. The pigments were mixed with a liquid (either milkweed sap, egg white, or animal fat) and applied with a feather or fiber brush.

There are many theories about the meaning of the rock art that the Chumash created. However, no one alive today can be certain about any of them. Some scholars believe that the paintings are maps or records that represent actual places, occurrences, or objects. Others believe they symbolize Chumash social laws and practices. Still others theorize that the paintings depict maps of the supernatural world or abstract figures of the Sky People. Regardless of their meaning, the artworks stand as some of the few special aspects of ancient Chumash ceremonial life.

The Chumash probably began to make rock paintings about 1,000 years ago, during a time of great industry, creativity, and economic growth in their nation. By this time, the number of people in the Chumash nation may have increased by as much as 5 times compared to the population of 3,000

A carved steatite killer whale effigy, approximately five inches long. Such animal effigies may have represented Chumash individuals' spirit guides.

Chumash rock paintings, inspired by Indians' sacred "journeys" to the spirit world. Today, native works of art such as this are threatened by vandalism. For example, several people have recently carved their initials into this group of designs.

years ago. The number and size of their villages and seasonal campsites grew as well.

By about A.D. 1500, the Chumash were producing more beads and luxury items than ever before, indicating a thriving society. The entire Chumash nation was joined together by a network of political and religious leaders, traders, and craft guilds. It was during this period that the Chumash first began to hear stories told by other Indian

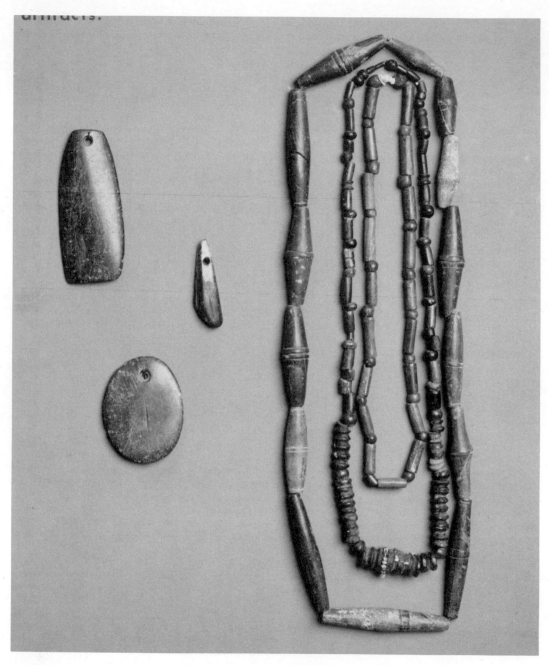

Pendants and a bead necklace intricately carved from steatite. The Chumash produced luxury items such as these primarily 1,000 to 2,000 years ago but during the early 16th century switched to shell-bead jewelry.

traders from Mexico about bearded strangers who traveled in huge seagoing vessels.

These were, for the most part, Spanish traders who were carrying supplies and trade goods to and from Spain's colonial outposts in Baja (Lower) and Alta (Upper) California. Spain had established a vast colonial empire in Mexico during the early decades of the 16th century and soon after made efforts to explore and stake out claims in what is now the southwestern United States. It was not long before the Chumash became acquainted with some of the participants in Spain's quest to expand its holdings and its influence in North America.

On October 10, 1542, the ships *La Victoria* and *San Salvador*, commanded by João Rodrigues Cabrilho (also known as Juan Cabrillo), a Portuguese explorer in the service of Spain, sailed into the Santa Barbara Channel at the heart of the Chumash homeland (part of Alta California) and dropped anchor. A small party of men, including Cabrilho, landed onshore and met with the members of a Chumash village, which he named Las Canoas (The Canoes) because the villagers possessed a large number of these boats. Although this meeting had little initial impact on the Chumash, it marked the beginning of the end of the Indians' traditional way of life. ▲

*An early-20th-century photograph of Lucrecía García, a young Bar-
bareño Chumash. She is dressed in the typical American dress of the
day, as most Chumash probably were.*

THE
MISSION ERA

The arrival of João Cabrilho and his men must have caused quite a stir among the Chumash, but at first the Spaniards' presence did not significantly change the Indians' daily way of life. Indeed, for almost 200 years afterward, the Chumash continued to live in much the same manner as they had before the Europeans arrived. The Indians had contacts with several more expeditions during those centuries, but these usually consisted of small groups of sailors who briefly stopped for water, wood, and food at the Chumash's island or mainland settlements. The majority of these oceangoing expeditions were either carrying goods to Spanish settlements or seeking a shortcut to the East. They therefore made no attempt to settle among the Chumash or to change the Indians' traditional culture.

In the mid-18th century, events began to take shape that would soon threaten the Chumash way of life. Although Spain had never considered Alta California a lucrative territory, the government did recognize its value as a buffer between Mexico and Spain's rivals, such as the British and the Russians, in the colonization of western North America. When these powers began funding expeditions that came closer and closer to Mexico, Spain was forced to take a stand. During the 1760s, the Spanish government embarked on a reform movement that included the consolidation under one official of its holdings in Mexico and the establishment of military and mission installations throughout Alta California.

The first outcome of this plan was the founding of Mission San Diego in April 1769. The leaders of the colonial expedition were Captain Gaspar de Portolá, the military leader, and Father Junípero Serra, a Franciscan priest and head of Spain's missions in Baja California. Each commanded a group of personnel who were to assist in the establishment of the mission. It was essential to the survival of the settlement, however, that the Indians in the surrounding villages be converted as soon as possible and trained to perform the necessary daily tasks at the missions. The missions received few supplies and were expected to become self-sufficient as quickly as they were able.

The Franciscan clergymen were not mercenary in their quest for Indian converts. The priests saw it as their duty to "save" the native people from what the Catholic church considered an unwholesome and unproductive existence. To them, the mission's use of Indian labor was simply a part of the church's plan to make useful citizens of the native inhabitants of Spain's colonial empire. However, they did not rule out forced conversion and harsh punishment as a means to achieve their goals. The Spanish colonial government was more than happy to support these activities because the converted Indians added to the citizenry of Spain's territory, making it more difficult for other nations to make claims to the land.

Although Mission San Diego was not an immediate success, the colonial government continued with its plans for Alta California. In August 1769, Captain Gaspar de Portolá set off northward from San Diego with a second Spanish expedition. The group included 27 soldiers, 7 muleteers, 2 Franciscan priests, and 15 Christianized Indians from Baja California. The expedition's main purpose was to find Monterey Bay, a potentially lucrative northern harbor described by Spanish sailors a hundred years earlier. The course of the journey took the team straight through the heart of Chumash territory.

The party stopped at many Chumash villages during its journey, and again the interaction between the Chumash and the Spanish was friendly. Usually small groups of Chumash would bring baskets filled with seeds, fruit, and dried and fresh fish and meat. In exchange, the Spanish offered glass beads, ribbon, or cloth, which were highly valued by the Chumash.

At least six people on the expedition kept a diary in which they recorded information about the route of the journey, the natural environment around them, and the practices of the Indians they encountered. These records included the appearance of the people, their manner of dress, the things they made, the design of their villages and houses, the foods they ate, and their customs and ceremonies. These diaries provide scholars with the first written record of the Chumash at a time when their culture was still unaffected by European influences.

At one village, the expedition was treated to a ceremonial dance, which they enjoyed, but they complained that the Indians continued the music and

A sketch by Russell A. Ruiz that depicts a welcoming party of Chumash in several tomols approaching the flagship of explorer João Cabrilho upon his arrival in Chumash territory in 1542.

dancing throughout the night. Indeed, Juan Crespi, one of the Franciscan friars, noted that "the Indians were quite kind but . . . they played weird flutes all night and kept us awake." Portolá named the settlement Ranchería del Baile de las Indias (Village of the Dancing Indians) in honor of its chief, whose dancing skills were much admired by the Spaniards. The Indians treated the travelers well during their stay and, upon their departure, pro-

LOCATION OF SPANISH MISSIONS IN CHUMASH TERRITORY

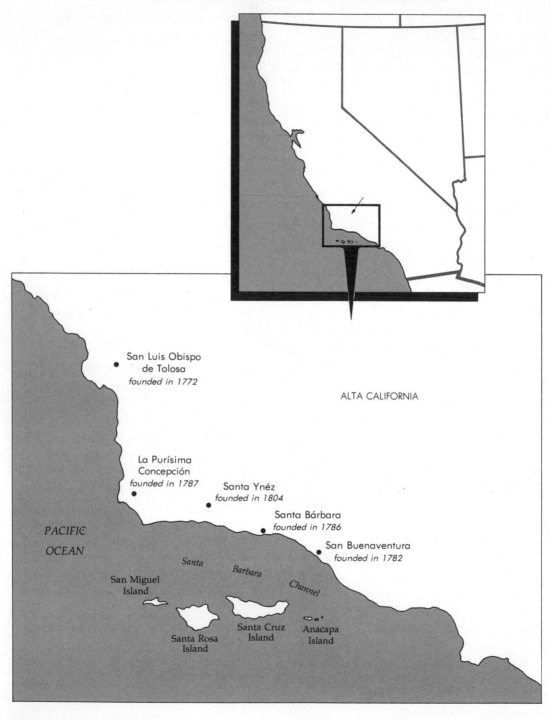

San Luis Obispo
de Tolosa
founded in 1772

ALTA CALIFORNIA

La Purísima
Concepción
founded in 1787

Santa Ynéz
founded in 1804

Santa Bárbara
founded in 1786

San Buenaventura
founded in 1782

PACIFIC

OCEAN

Santa

Barbara

Channel

San Miguel
Island

Santa Rosa
Island

Santa Cruz
Island

Anacapa
Island

vided them with stores of food and water for their journey.

During its five-month journey, the Portolá expedition traveled through most of the coastal Chumash settlements. The explorers did not succeed in their search for Monterey Bay, but they found something of equal value. At each village, the group was invariably welcomed wholeheartedly by the Indians, a response that led the Spanish government to believe that they would have little difficulty in claiming and settling the region. As a result, the Spanish crown funded a second trip, also led by Portolá, in search of the bay. This time he found it.

In May 1770, Gaspar de Portolá arrived at Monterey Bay and claimed it in the name of Spain. He was soon followed by an expedition that included Junípero Serra, who had been appointed to oversee the construction and operation of a mission at Monterey. Two years later, having accomplished those tasks, Serra made a trip southward into Chumash territory. He stopped at what is now the city of San Luis Obispo, erected a cross and a bell, and consecrated Mission San Luis Obispo de Tolosa, the first Franciscan mission in Chumash territory. During the next 30 years, the Spanish government authorized the construction of 4 more missions—San Buenaventura in 1782, Santa Bárbara in 1786, La Purísima Concepción in 1787, and Santa Ynéz in 1804.

During their early years, the missions were relatively insubstantial settlements, sometimes consisting only of an altar and a few shelters for the military and church personnel and the very few Indian converts. For example, Mission San Luis Obispo de Tolosa had only two Chumash members. The first Chumash to enter the missions were often sick or dying children or poor families who did so in order to receive food and other goods.

The Chumash probably began coming to the missions simply to trade for European goods, such as metal tools and utensils. Indeed, the settlements, such as Mission Santa Bárbara, were often established within a few miles of large Chumash rancherías. The clergymen may have assumed that their presence among the Chumash would be enough to convince them to give up their traditions and embrace Chrisianity. When it became clear that this was not the case, the priests began a campaign, carried out by the military, to capture as many Chumash as they could and force the Indians to live and work at the missions.

Most of the missions were similar in design and function. Each consisted of a church, living quarters for the priests, soldiers, and baptized Indians, storage houses, workshops, and agricultural plots. The structures commonly varied in size from 25 square feet to more than 300 square feet. Some of the largest buildings measured 1,000 square feet and were divided into many small rooms.

The buildings were constructed from adobe bricks, wood beams that held up the ceiling, and roofs made of

A painting of Mission San Gabriel Arcangel, by Oriana Day. Most of the Indians in California were forced to perform virtual slave labor for the missionaries.

tule mats or clay tile. Adobe bricks and tiles were made by mixing clay, straw, and water together and then packing the mixture into wooden molds. The cakes were dried in the sun and then removed from the molds. The result was a rectangular brick or tile that was almost as hard as stone.

When the Indians were brought to the missions, they were forced to give up all their traditional practices for those of Spanish society. The new converts, known as neophytes, were baptized, instructed in the teachings of Catholicism, and taught trades that would assist the priests and soldiers in the daily operation of the mission. These tasks included farming, animal husbandry, pottery making, weaving, iron working, masonry, and irrigation.

An intricate basketry box made by Chumash during the mission era.

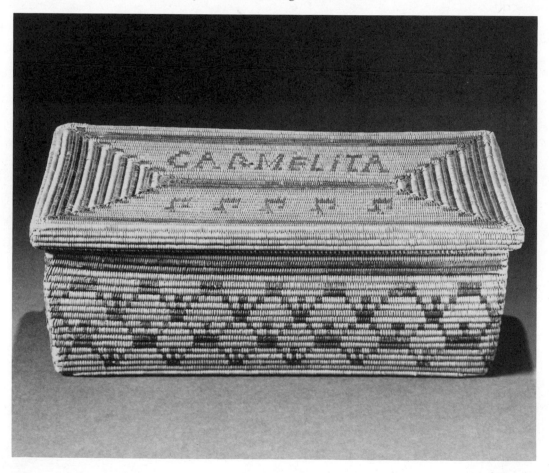

Indeed, Indians provided almost all the labor required to construct and maintain the Spanish mission system throughout California. The priests and soldiers served as managers and instructors and performed little actual labor.

The daily routines of mission life were far different from those of traditional Chumash culture, and the Indians found them alien and tedious. In the late 18th century, a church scholar described a typical day at a mission:

> Half an hour after sunrise, having taken their breakfast of atole [a cereal], the neophytes assemble in the church to hear holy Mass, during which they recite the catechism . . . in their language. From the church they go to their homes, take up their implements and work until half past eleven. Then they take their meal, which consists of boiled wheat, corn, peas, beans. Then they rest until two o'clock, in winter until three at which time they go to work at their tasks until an hour before sunset. They then take their supper . . . as in the morning, return to church to recite the . . . catechism, and sing. Having finished the function of the church, they return to their homes.

The regulations set down by the mission priests were far different from those that had governed Chumash towns. The most striking of these differences was the priests' segregation of unmarried Chumash men and women, which began when they reached the age of 11. The members of each sex had to eat and sleep in separate (usually overcrowded) quarters. The unmarried women were forced to sleep in a building that was kept locked throughout the night.

Furthermore, the Chumash were fed a diet that was far less palatable and much less nutritious than was provided by the foods they had traditionally eaten. In fact, they were usually fed the same thing—atole—at virtually every meal, although they were occasionally given meat or fish. At some of the missions, however, some of the neophytes were permitted to return to their former villages to visit relatives. While at home, the Indians often collected traditional resources, hunted for game, and fished to supplement the insufficient amount of food they received at the missions.

Besides European laws, customs, and religious practices, the Spaniards had unknowingly brought with them deadly diseases. Over time, the Europeans had developed immunities to such plagues as measles, smallpox, pneumonia, and mumps. However, the Chumash had had no such opportunity, and the cramped conditions at the missions only helped to increase the rapid spread of infection. They died by the thousands. Indeed, the entire population of California Indians had dropped from 300,000 to only about 30,000 by the early 19th century. As a result, most villages were abandoned, and more and more people sought refuge either with distant relatives or with the missionaries.

Once all of Alta California was in Spanish hands, the missionaries felt that they no longer needed to worry about the consequences of mistreating their converts. The Spanish government, turning a blind eye to reports of ill-treatment of neophytes at the missions, helped to support this belief. Spain's primary concern was that its colonial holdings in Alta California be maintained, no matter what the cost to the native peoples there. Indeed, when the Franciscan friar Antonio de la Concepción Horra reported that "for the slightest things the [Indians] receive heavy floggings, are shackled, and put in the stocks, and treated with so much cruelty that they are kept whole days without a drink of water," he was declared insane and placed under arrest.

It is not surprising that many of the Chumash began to rebel against their terrible living conditions. The first of such incidents occurred in 1801 at Mission Santa Bárbara after a Chumash woman received a vision from the Chumash deity Chupu. The spirit instructed her to tell all of the Chumash (whether they had been baptized or not) that they must reject the ways of the Spanish and return to their traditions. This happened during a devastating pneumonia and pleurisy outbreak, which lent great weight to the movement. However, an informer leaked news of the impending rebellion to the clergymen, who quickly subdued the rebels.

Despite such instances of resistance, the number of Chumash at the missions increased during 1802 and 1803 (the latter year saw the highest population figure ever). The most probable explanation for this unlikely situation was that disease, land loss, and starvation in the Indians' villages and towns left them with no choice but to enter the mission system. By this time, most of the Indians' traditional leadership was disrupted, as were their craft guilds, religious institutions, and family relationships.

By February 1824, conditions had become so bad that the Chumash at Mission La Purísima Concepción and Mission Santa Bárbara staged revolts. The rebellions were initially sparked by a severe beating given to one of the neophytes at Mission Santa Ynéz, but this act merely inflamed an already growing feeling of anger and dissension among the Chumash. They banded together and burned and sacked much of the mission's property. Soon after, a war party of some 200 Chumash took over Mission La Purísima Concepción, and their number increased to 400 when they were joined by warriors from other missions.

Within a matter of days, news of the revolt reached the Chumash at Mission Santa Bárbara and they in turn rose up. However, events did not go quite so well for the Chumash at Santa Bárbara. They became engaged in armed conflict with the Spanish military at the mission, and several Chumash were killed during the fighting. However, the Chu-

An early-20th-century photograph of a Chumash couple at Mission Santa Bárbara.

mash gained the upper hand, and after destroying and plundering much of the mission, they sought refuge in the hills to the east.

It took more than a month for the Franciscan and military leaders to form a plan for retaliation. Had such a revolt happened in the 1800s, the situation might have been resolved quickly and with harsh consequences for the Chumash. At this time, however, the Mexican government was engaged in a struggle with Spain for control of the colony, so the government was unable to provide much aid to the missions. Mexico did agree, however, that the

Chumash could not be allowed to succeed in their rebellion because it would threaten the economic structure of Alta California—a structure based on Indian labor. Therefore, both the mission leadership and the Mexican government agreed that the most important immediate goal was to recapture Mission La Purísima.

The colonial leaders first decided to send more than 100 mounted, heavily armed soldiers to take on the Chumash defenders. On March 16, 1824, the war party reached the mission and began to fire on it. The Chumash answered with their own stores of ammunition—muskets, cannons, and arrows. The battle went on for most of the morning, with little prospect of victory for either side. Finally, the two groups agreed to a cease-fire that was negotiated with the aid of the priests. In the aftermath, criminal prosecution was brought against the Chumash leaders of the rebellion: At least 7 were executed, and 4 others were sentenced to 10 years of hard labor.

The Mexican government was presented with a greater difficulty in its attempts at recapturing the Chumash who fled from Mission Santa Bárbara. The Mexicans knew that the mission could not be run without the use of Indian labor, but they also knew that they would never be able to round up all of the escapees and bring them back to the mission. The government's initial reaction was to chase the Chumash down and try to intimidate them into return-

ing. In April, the soldiers encountered a force of Chumash in the San Joaquin Valley. The two sides engaged in a brief battle, during which several Indians were killed. The Mexicans, however, were unable to capture the rest of the Chumash, who fled farther inland.

The situation was finally resolved when the Mexican military leaders negotiated a truce with the Chumash. The Indians agreed to return to the mission only after they forced the Mexicans to allow them to keep their arms. However, even this concession was not enough to convince a great number of Chumash, who refused to return to the mission and continued to live in the Sierra Madre as best they could.

The Indian rebellions (and there were many others besides those of the Chumash) of the early 19th century were resolved, for the most part, in the missions' favor. However, the system was unable to regain its former total control of the Indians. Throughout the late 1820s and early 1830s, the population of mission Indians continued to decline as a result of escape and of death, particularly of infants. Indeed, some sources report that Chumash women practiced infanticide in order to spare their children the miseries of mission life.

These sad conditions persisted until 1833, when a new form of administration came to control the lives of the Chumash. In that year, the Mexican government removed the missions from the jurisdiction of the Catholic church and turned them over to private citizens and governmental administrators. For some Chumash, this signaled a time for regaining some of their traditions and their autonomy. For others, it merely marked another episode in the many years of labor for which the Chumash gained little or no reward. ▲

Chumash historian, singer, and storyteller Vincent Tumamait, photographed by Ivan Hunter in 1989 at the "Chumash Today" program sponsored by the Santa Barbara Museum of Natural History.

AFTER
THE
SPANISH

After the missions were placed in government and private hands, increasing numbers of Mexicans began to migrate to Alta California in order to take advantage of the new land openings. However, the Mexican government had taken steps to ensure that the mission Indians would not be left without land or be forced to become servants of the incoming settlers. In 1827, the Mexican constitution gave the mission Indians the right to move as they pleased and encouraged them to become productive members of Mexican society. During the process of secularization, the governor of Mexico, José Figueroa, enacted further legislation to protect the mission Indians, including the Chumash. Known as the Provisional Regulation for the Emancipation of the Mission Indians, this 1833 act stated that one-half of the missions' property was to be divided among the Indians who had lived at each mission. The land was to be held in trust for the Indians by the mission administrators.

Unfortunately, Figueroa's plan did not work out the way he had intended. By the late 1830s, most of the land that had been designated as Chumash property had been taken over by Mexican settlers and consolidated into huge estates known as ranchos. Much of the Indians' land was lost because families were unable to make an adequate living on their plots, which were usually too small to be productive. The Figueroa act forbade the Chumash to sell or consolidate their individual farmsteads, so many simply abandoned them. Some of these dispossessed Indians stayed at the now-tiny missions and lived off the meager resources of the clergymen. Others went to small towns to look for wage work or moved to the interior to live among the unconverted tribes there.

The majority of the landless Chumash remained on the former mission lands as employees of the new Mexican owners. Most of the Chumash had been born and raised at the missions and knew little of any other way of life. The skills that had made the Indians valuable to the Franciscans made them equally useful to the rancheros, as the Mexican owners were known. Therefore, most of the mission Indians simply traded one group of masters for another. But unlike the Franciscans, who at least had had the Indians' spiritual welfare in mind, the rancheros operated solely on the motive of increasing their wealth. To them, the Chumash merely represented a means to that end.

The ranchos were unlike the missions in other significant ways as well. For example, all of the supplies and daily necessities that were used at the missions were, for the most part, made there. On the ranchos, however, work was concentrated on the production and maintenance of vast cattle herds. All other supplies were purchased from American traders with the money acquired from beef sales. As a result, the Indians who worked on the ranchos

Ventureño Chumash Donna Guiterras, photographed in the early 20th century.

Fernando Librado standing in front of a brush shelter that he built as a demonstration model for John P. Harrington.

soon lost all of the agricultural and do-mestic skills in which they had been trained at the missions. The Chumash had also been permitted by the Fran-ciscans to leave the missions for occa-sional visits to their former villages, enabling them to keep their traditions alive to some degree. On the ranchos, however, the Chumash were kept un-der constant surveillance and were never allowed to leave. They soon lost almost all connection to their former way of life.

For those Chumash who fled to the interior, the Mexican period was a deadly time. These Indians and their allies from other tribes had moved to the mountains—out of reach of Mexi-can settlers. While living in these high-lands, many of them had acquired and learned to use horses from eastern tribes. These Chumash survived mainly by farming, hunting, and raiding cattle and horses from the ranchos on the easternmost edge of Mexican settlement.

The raiding activities of the Chumash and other Indians aroused the anger of the Mexicans. As a result, during the late 1830s and early 1840s, Mexican military parties conducted a campaign to annihilate the Chumash for their actions. The Mexican leaders in Alta California sponsored raids on the Indians' villages during which the soldiers often slaughtered almost all of the Indian inhabitants, even small children and infants. Those youngsters that were not killed were often taken from their homes and sold to rancheros as slaves.

Throughout the period of Mexican control in Alta California, European-introduced diseases continued to kill Indians by the thousands. During a particularly deadly epidemic in 1833, at least 4,500 Indians died. Indeed, the population of California Indians, which had begun to increase at the end of the mission period, fell by more than 60 percent during the Mexican occupation.

Alta California's distance from the Mexican central government and the increasing and costly skirmishes with Indian groups began to take a toll on the colony in the mid-19th century. These factors, combined with the increasing numbers of American settlers traveling to the area, eventually forced Mexico to relinquish its hold on Alta California. Hostilities between the United States and Mexico, now known as the Mexican War, continued during the late 1840s because of the United States's annexation of Texas and incursions into California. In 1848, the conflict was resolved by the Treaty of Guadalupe Hidalgo, which granted possession of Alta California as well as portions of New Mexico and Arizona to the victorious United States in return for $15 million.

The United States takeover of Alta California signaled the end for many of the Indian cultures in the region. Whereas the Spanish and the Mexicans had at least kept the Indians alive to use as cheap labor, the incoming American settlers, for the most part, wanted them off the land and out of the way. Soon after the treaty with Mexico, gold was discovered in central California, bringing thousands of pioneers to the region. These settlers were merely looking for quick profits in the gold fields at first, but few managed to find them. Many decided to remain anyway and soon established farms, ranches, and towns. The number of Americans in the territory grew so rapidly that by 1850 California had become the 31st state of the Union.

With the missions and ranchos gone, there were not even minimal laws to protect the Chumash from white persecution. The Indians were considered wards of the U.S. government and as such were unable to legally defend themselves in court or take action against atrocities committed by American settlers. As a result, almost all of the Chumash were quickly forced off

A Chumash man dressed in the ritual clothing of a swordfish dancer. The performer studied several museum collections in order to re-create the garments worn during the 2,000-year-old ceremony. The dance was traditionally performed in order to honor swordfish, believed by the Chumash to drive ashore whales, a coveted resource.

any productive land that they owned. Racist views of Indians were common among the settlers, who viewed the Chumash either as wild savages who ought to be destroyed or as less than fully human creatures who deserved only ridicule and pity. One U.S. official who studied the condition of California Indians noted, "I have seldom heard of a single difficulty between the whites and the Indians in which the original cause could not readily be traced to some rash or reckless act of the former."

The U.S. government had little control over the problems between Indians and whites in the early years of California's statehood. In fact, word of many of the atrocities committed against the Indians rarely even reached Washington. Most of the officials sent out to oversee the treatment of the Chumash and other tribes quickly became corrupted. They were either bribed by the wealthy landowners and businessmen in the region or were simply overcome by the ease of falsifying requests and appropriating supplies and funds that were intended for the Indians.

When the Indians retaliated against the whites' ill treatment, military campaigns were organized against them by the state government. As a result, the federal government, which might have favored mediation between the two groups, usually did not find out about hostilities until it was too late to correct them. These campaigns were often wildly excessive and shockingly brutal in their punishment of the Indians. In

1850, a witness described a military action:

> [The soldiers] went across [the lake] in their long dug-outs, the [I]ndians said they would meet them in peace. So when the whites landed the [I]ndians went to wellcom them but the white man was determined to kill them. [One man] threw up his hands and [asked the soldiers not to harm him] but the white man fired and shoot [sic] him in the arm. One old lady . . . saw two white men coming with their guns up in the air and on their guns hung a little girl, they brought [her] to the creek and threw [her] in the water . . . two more men came . . . and this time they had a little boy on the end of their guns and also threw [him] in the water.

By the 1850s, the formerly vast and powerful Chumash nation was reduced to several small groups, with only 100 or so Indians living at the Santa Ynéz mission. The rest survived on scant resources in the interior or suffered humiliation, starvation, and persecution as wage laborers and domestic servants to whites. Few of them were able to gather any of their traditional food resources because white farmers had destroyed or fenced in all of the Chumash's former food-collecting sites. Many were forced into slavery after the California legislature passed a law that made it possible for Indians to be declared vagrants (without proof and by any white person who wished to do so), imprisoned, and then sold at auction as unpaid laborers for a specific number of weeks or months. The legislation also allowed Indian parents to "sell" their children to employers for a certain number of years, during which they worked only for food and shelter.

In 1901, some Chumash were provided with a small means to make a living. In that year, the U.S. government ceded to the Chumash 75 acres of reserved land located next to the Santa Ynéz mission on Zanja de Cota Creek. However, the acreage of the reservation was too small to support many families. There were usually fewer than 50 permanent residents on the tribal land, although that number increased to almost

A group of Chumash men, photographed in 1976, paddle a modern-day re-creation of a traditional canoe. The men constructed the canoe as part of a celebration commemorating the 1776 arrival in Chumash territory of an expedition headed by the Spanish explorer Juan Bautista de Anza.

Peter Zavala, dressed in traditional Chumash dancing garments and ornaments, and his daughter Takaita, photographed in 1989 at the "Chumash Today" program.

100 during the second half of the 20th century. Today, all people of at least one-quarter Chumash ancestry have lived on the reservation at some point in their life, but movement on and off the land is frequent.

During most of the 20th century, the Chumash maintained some aspects of their traditional culture. They continued to burn the possessions of deceased tribe members and to wail during funerals. The Chumash, for the most part, chose marriage partners from among tribe members, although there was and continues to be some inter-marriage with Mexican Americans and other ethnic groups.

In general, the Chumash gradually came to resemble the Mexican-American Catholics who lived in the villages and towns surrounding the reservation. Since the death of the last fluent Chumash speakers in the 1920s, the first language of almost all Chumash has been Spanish, but many speak English as well. Most Chumash are members of the Catholic church. Attendance, however, is usually restricted to funerals and baptisms.

Most Chumash families on the reservation consist of several closely related individuals, usually headed by a woman, her children, and sometimes one or both of her parents. In order to earn money, many Chumash women either work as domestic servants in nearby towns or grow and sell vegetables on their land. Chumash men must often seek work off the reservation, often outside of the town of Santa Ynez.

Education among the Chumash has been erratic. In the very early years of the 20th century, the U.S. government ran a school on the reservation, but it was in operation for only a short time. After it closed, Chumash children attended the public school at Santa Ynez, where they became the first generation to speak English. In the 1930s and early 1940s, six or seven children who successfully completed elementary school were sent to the Sherman Institute in Riverside, California. There they received high school instruction and vocational training. However, this school closed in 1948, and Chumash teenagers were sent to the local high school at Santa Ynez.

There have been and remain many factors at work against Chumash children in the public schools. In the early years, Chumash students were the victims of prejudice because of their lack of English and their Indian ancestry. Although most completed elementary school, many children did not and do not attend high school at all. Some may have stayed for a year or so. Today, the students' reasons for dropping out include illness, problems at home that require the child's presence, and a need to work in order to raise money for the family.

When the Chumash were granted the Santa Ynez Reservation, they altered their political structure in order to better deal with the U.S. government. Tribal affairs are now controlled by the 5-member Chumash Business Council, whose members are elected every 2 years, and a general council that is made up of all tribe members over the age of 21. The Chumash Business Council has overseen the establishment of a bingo enterprise and the implementation of a federal housing program.

The only land officially held by the Chumash today is the federally granted Santa Ynez Reservation, which now consists of about 75 acres. Located on the reservation land are the homes of several Chumash families and a hall that is used for tribal meetings and gatherings. The reservation hosts a number of social events during the year. During these festivals, traditional foods are served, and dances and other cultural activities are conducted for the benefit of the Chumash, other Native Americans, and the general public. Many of the Chumash also demonstrate traditional dances at various non-Indian community events. Some tribe members give lectures about native philosophy and ways of life, both past and present, and teach traditional arts and crafts at public schools and colleges throughout the United States.

There are a number of Chumash who do not live on the reservation but continue to maintain their cultural identity. Many of them are active in one or more Chumash cultural societies and groups, such as the United Chumash Council (UCC), the Brotherhood of the Tomol, the Southern Owl Clan, and the Ventura United Chumash. These groups actively participate in and fight for the preservation, maintenance, and survival of sacred and historic sites throughout the traditional Chumash region.

These Chumash groups and the inhabitants of the Santa Ynez Reservation are extremely diligent in learning the archaeological techniques and legal and political strategies for preserving their heritage. In this regard, they have sponsored special education classes on the reservation during which invited scholars have instructed them in archaeological methods and theories and in Chumash history. With this newly acquired knowledge, many of the Chumash have served as computer analysts and field and laboratory assistants to archaeologists and other scholars conducting research into Chumash culture.

Since the early 1970s, federal and state environmental laws have helped to protect Chumash cultural resources, including sacred religious places, traditional sites of villages and camps, cemeteries, wetlands, and important plant areas. These laws require developers to ensure that no damage will come to sacred places and natural resources during construction projects. In compliance with these restrictions, developers hire archaeologists to conduct surveys of the areas and to identify important cultural resources, such as cemeteries, sacred places, or historic villages. This process is known as cultural resource management, or CRM work.

When conducting CRM work, archaeologists must also include the concerns of the Chumash community.

Chumash Juanita Centeno demonstrates traditional craft-making techniques at the "Chumash Today" program in Santa Barbara.

Vincent Tumamait, who is of Cuyama, Ventureño, and Cruzano Chumash ancestry, poses with Barbareño Chumash Ernestine de Soto McGovran (center) and Obispeño Chumash Lei Lynn Olivas Odom (left).

Most important among these are the protection of historic and prehistoric villages, camps, native plants, animals, mineral resources, and burial and spiritual sites. During most surveys and excavations, Chumash representatives are hired to oversee the work and to ensure that damage to the sites and the surrounding natural environment is minimal. These observers take daily notes and make monthly reports to the Chumash Business Council.

The Chumash also have a representative on the California Native Heritage Commission. This person must be contacted in the event that a Chumash burial is uncovered, because such sites are sacred and are protected by California law from disturbance. When a surveyor makes such a discovery, he or she must request that the Chumash council member come to the site. The council member will then ensure that the burial is protected from further damage and make arrangements for an official reburial.

In 1988, the U.S. government demonstrated to the Chumash the respect and concern that the scientific community holds for their culture. During the late 1980s, Vandenberg Air Force Base, which is located in traditional Chumash territory, was chosen as the site for a space shuttle launch. When the first shuttle was sent to the base, the government contacted the Chumash in order to inform them of the event. In response, the tribe sent out a representative who, accompanied by an archaeologist, walked ahead of the truck that was towing the shuttle to ensure that no damage came to any of the Chumash sites along the sides of the road.

In the past 20 years, Chumash in most parts of their nation have joined together into many organizations designed to help their community with health, jobs, and cultural matters and to interact with developers and government officials on cultural resource matters. The Chumash of today are prominent spokespeople for many environmental issues facing the people of California and the rest of the world. They have lived in balance with their surroundings for thousands of years, and they realize that this balance must be maintained if cultures are to survive and prosper. In this way, they continue their spiritual and cultural relationship with their ancient homeland while embracing the issues that affect their life as 20th-century Americans. ▲

BIBLIOGRAPHY

Bean, L. J., and Thomas C. Blackburn, eds. *Native Californians: A Theoretical Perspective*. Ramona, CA: Ballena Press/Santa Barbara Museum of Natural History Cooperative, 1976.

Blackburn, Thomas C., ed. *December's Child: A Book of Chumash Oral Narratives*. Berkeley: University of California Press, 1975.

Grant, Campbell. *The Rock Paintings of the Chumash: A Study of Californian Indian Culture*. Berkeley: University of California Press, 1965.

Heizer, Robert F., ed. *California Handbook of North American Indians*. Vol. 8. Washington, D.C.: Smithsonian Institution, 1978.

Hudson, Travis, and Thomas C. Blackburn. *The Material Culture of the Chumash Interaction Sphere*. Vols. 1–5. Ramona, CA: Ballena Press/Santa Barbara Museum of Natural History Cooperative, 1979.

King, Chester D. *The Evolution of Chumash Society: A Comparative Study of Artifacts Used in Social System Maintenance in the Santa Barabara Channel Region Before A.D. 1804*. Ann Arbor, MI: University Microfilms, 1982.

Kroeber, A. L. *Handbook of the Indians of California*. Berkeley: California Book Co., Ltd., 1953.

Landberg, Leif C. W. *The Chumash Indians of Southern California*. Los Angeles: Southwest Museum, 1965.

THE CHUMASH AT A GLANCE

CULTURE AREA   *California*

GEOGRAPHY   *The coast of what is now California from Malibu Creek in Los Angeles County to San Carpojo Creek in San Luis Obispo County*

LINGUISTIC FAMILY   *Hokan*

CURRENT POPULATION   *Approximately 5,000*

FIRST CONTACT   *João Rodrigues Cabrilho, Spanish, 1542*

FEDERAL STATUS   *Only the Chumash living on the Santa Ynez Reservation are recognized by the federal government. However, several other organizations and regional councils are recognized by the California Native American Heritage Commission.*

GLOSSARY

adobe A brick or building material of sun-dried earth and straw. Adobe also refers to the structures made of this material.

agriculture Intensive cultivation of tracts of land, sometimes using draft animals and heavy plowing equipment. Agriculture requires a largely nonnomadic life.

allotment U.S. policy applied nationwide through the General Allotment Act passed in 1887, aimed at breaking up tribally owned reservations by assigning individual farms and ranches to Indians. Allotment was intended as much to discourage traditional communal activities as to encourage private farming and assimilate Indians into mainstream American life.

antap A Chumash religious cult. Members were keepers of sacred knowledge, including dances, songs, and rituals, and performed these during fiestas. Because members' families paid a large fee, only the wealthiest Chumash were included in the antap.

anthropology The study of the physical, social, and historical characteristics of human beings.

anthropomorphic Resembling or similar to a human figure, humanlike, or endowed with human characteristics.

archaeologist A scientist who studies past human societies through the objects, records, and settlements that people leave behind.

archaeology The recovery and reconstruction of human ways of life through the study of material culture (including tools, clothing, and food and human remains).

asphaltum A naturally occurring, gluey tar used by the Chumash for many purposes, such as fixing utensils, waterproofing canoes and baskets, and attaching stone points to wooden handles.

band A loosely organized group of people who are bound together by the need for food and defense, by family ties, and/or by other common interests.

clan A multigenerational group having a shared identity, organization, and property based on belief in descent from a common ancestor. Because clan members consider themselves closely related, marriage within a clan is strictly prohibited.

culture The learned behavior of humans; nonbiological, socially taught activities; the way of life of a group of people.

Emancipation of Mission Indians The 1833 act passed by the Mexican government stating that one-half of a mission's property was to be divided among the Indians who had lived at that mission. The land was held in trust for the Indians by the mission administrators.

fiesta A gathering attended by people from each Chumash village. During fiestas, people traded and sold goods, played games, and performed rituals, and village leaders discussed problems and upcoming events.

Franciscan A member of the Order of Friars Minor, a Roman Catholic order founded by St. Francis of Assisi in 1209. The Franciscans are dedicated to preaching, missionary work, and charitable acts.

metate A flat slab of rock on which a Chumash woman ground seeds, nuts, and other plant foods into flour using a round, hand-held stone known as a mano.

Mexican War A conflict between the United States and Mexico that lasted from 1846 to 1848. The Mexican War resulted from the United States's annexation of Texas and its incursion into California.

mission A religious center founded by advocates of a particular denomination who are trying to convert nonbelievers to their faith.

neophytes Indians who were converted to Christianity and made to live and work at a mission.

olivella The shell of a marine animal from which the Chumash manufactured their shell-bead currency.

patrilineal descent Rules for determining family or clan membership by tracing kinship through male ancestors.

paxa A Chumash ceremonial leader, whose responsibilities included making announcements and giving speeches, directing fiesta events, preparing the sacred ceremonial dancing grounds, and collecting offerings for the tribal leader.

pit house A dwelling that consisted of a dome-shaped pole framework constructed over a pit dug a few feet into the ground.

ranchería The Spanish word for an Indian village, in colonial California.

ranchos Estates made up of land that originally belonged to either the Chumash or the missions. Ranchos were owned by wealthy bureaucrats and merchants.

reservation, reserve A tract of land retained by Indians for their own occupation and use. *Reservation* is used to describe such lands in the United States; *reserve*, in Canada.

secularization A process by which the Mexican government took control of the California missions away from the Franciscans and turned it over to the head of each mission. Through a provision written into the Mexican constitution in 1827, the Mexican government gave the neophyte Indians the right to move from place to place, thus encouraging them to become productive members of Mexican society.

shaman A Chumash medicine man, who was mainly responsible for curing disease, combating illness, and contacting the spiritual world. Shamans also had the power to interpret dreams and forecast or avert storms and the responsibility of naming children.

siliyik A special dance enclosure erected at certain times of the year on the ceremonial grounds of a Chumash village. Only certain people were allowed to witness sacred dances, so siliyiks were surrounded by a high wall of woven bulrush mats that was hung with feathered banners.

soaproot A plant used by the Chumash for a variety of purposes. Depending on how it was prepared, soaproot could be used as a poison for paralyzing fish, as a coating for tool handles, as a cleansing agent, and as a nutritious food.

temescal The Spanish name for a Chumash sweathouse, constructed so as to seal in the heat from the central fire. They were used exclusively by Chumash men for both religious and nonreligious purposes, including purifying the body of disease and bad spirits. In the temescales, Chumash men would also talk, sing, or prepare themselves mentally and physically for a hunt.

territory A defined region of the United States that is not, but may become, a state. The government officials of a territory are appointed by the president, but territory residents elect their own legislature.

tok Milkweed fiber used to make string for a bow.

toloache A hallucinogenic drink made from the jimsonweed plant. The Chumash drank toloache in order to induce a dream state in which a person contacted his or her spiritual guide in the spirit world.

tomol Also known as a plank canoe, a tomol was made from driftwood boards that had holes drilled in them, allowing the planks to be sewn together. This unique type of canoe took up to six months to build.

treaty A contract negotiated between representatives of the United States government or another national government and one or more Indian tribes. Treaties dealt with the cessation of military action, the surrender of political independence, the establishment of boundaries, terms of land sales, and related matters.

Treaty of Guadalupe Hidalgo The 1848 agreement between Mexico and the United States that ended the Mexican War. The treaty granted to the United States possession of Alta California as well as portions of New Mexico and Arizona.

tribe A society consisting of several or many separate communities united by kinship, culture, language, and other social institutions including clans, religious organizations, and warrior societies.

trust The relationship between the federal government and many Indian tribes, dating from the late 19th century. Government agents managed Indians' business dealings, including land transactions and rights to national resources, because the Indians were considered legally incompetent to manage their own affairs.

wot The Chumash word for chief. A wot held the highest social position in the class structure of a Chumash village.

PICTURE CREDITS

ROBERT O. GIBSON, a lifelong resident of central California, received his B.A. in anthropology from the University of California, Los Angeles, and his M.A. in anthropology from California State University, Hayward. He has worked extensively in southern and central California specializing in Chumash prehistory and culture. An expert in both preindustrial technology and primitive economics, he has published articles on prehistoric and historic shell beads and ornaments and written numerous archaeological technical reports. For the past two decades he has worked as a private consultant for local, state, and federal agencies. Working with Chumash organizations and teaching classes in archaeological methods and techniques, he has contributed significantly to the preservation of archaeological resources.

FRANK W. PORTER III, general editor of INDIANS OF NORTH AMERICA, is director of the Chelsea House Foundation for American Indian Studies. He holds a B.A., M.A., and Ph.D. from the University of Maryland. He has done extensive research concerning the Indians of Maryland and Delaware and is the author of numerous articles on their history, archaeology, geography, and ethnography. He was formerly director of the Maryland Commission on Indian Affairs and American Indian Research and Resource Institute, Gettysburg, Pennsylvania, and he has received grants from the Delaware Humanities Forum, the Maryland Committee for the Humanities, the Ford Foundation, and the National Endowment for the Humanities, among others. Dr. Porter is the author of The Bureau of Indian Affairs in the Chelsea House KNOW YOUR GOVERNMENT series.